THE GROVE OF DANA

Ovate Course

NEW ORDER OF DRUIDS

OVATE COURSE

Published by Lulu.com
ISBN: 978-1-365-48181-9

Photo cover from istockphoto.com

Ovate Course, by Jason Kirkey - Copyright 2006 Druidcircle.net. All rights reserved.

First edition 2007 – Cafepress.com

Second edition 2016 – Lulu.com

Contents

The Well of Segais:
AN INTRODUCTION TO THE OVATE COURSE

In native Irish sources there is a story revolving around the Otherworldly ordeals of perhaps the most famous king in Irish literature, Cormac Mac Art. During these ordeals he finds himself in the Otherworldly *Land of Truth*, the realm of Manannan MacLir, a god of the sea, and thus keeper of the veils between this world and the Otherworld.

Here, Cormac sees the Well of Segais. There are five streams flowing forth from the well, and around the well are nine hazel trees. Within the water are five purple-bellied salmon. Every so often a hazelnut drops from the trees only to be eaten by one of the salmon in the well.

Manannan explains to Cormac that this is the Well of Wisdom (hazels and salmons both being symbolic of wisdom in the Irish tradition), and that each stream issuing forth from it is one of the five physical senses. All people drink from the five streams, but only poets, seers, druids; the *aos dana*, the gifted or skilled ones, drink from both the streams and the well itself.

This is a potent symbol and one which I feel encapsulates, to some extent, the journey of the Ovate course. One of the goals of this course is to facilitate an opening of the senses; both the physical senses, and the non-ordinary senses. The story of the Well of Segais is essentially about this task. It is important to note that the streams of the five senses come directly from the well itself, and that everyone must drink from these. The physical senses are a viable pathway to wisdom, and to the awakening of the non-ordinary senses of the *aos dana*, who drink from both the streams *and* the well itself. We might envision the streams as roads, taking us to the well, or from our world to the Otherworld.

The modern world has largely dulled our senses, ordinary and non-ordinary. When we stop using our senses they atrophy, and this is exactly what has happened. Industrial society creates the illusion that we no longer need our senses, but because we no longer depend on them in the same way to survive. The slow crunch of leaves, or the scent on the breeze, no longer signals that our prey or predator is nearby. Even our understanding of the sensuous has been distorted.

The body is where we perceive from, and it is the direct physical experience of nature that lies at the heart of nature mysticism and druidism. It is not just about speaking with the spirits of nature. Sometimes the simple act of listening to the physical sound of a flowing stream *is* the mysticism, without projecting our own ego's need of the mysterious and spiritual into the experience. Being present is often enough, and by attempting to over-spiritualize the world we end up simply blocking our own direct experience.

This is not to say that there are not real spiritual presences inhabiting the landscape with us; it does not mean that the world is not vibrant and dripping with the dew of a conscious, living, and enlivening presence. It is. But this enlivening, this presence of mystery and beauty is far more likely to appear to us in the slow falling of leaves in autumn, the gracious warmth of the sun on a cold day, the touch of water to dry lips, and the soil that yearns for our bare feet – than it is to come to us as an unignorable booming voice from the heavens. Soul and nature are more often than not subtle, and it is the soft gaze of the awakened senses that reveal the invisible presence of the Otherworld.

This course is about walking the pathway of the senses, the *sacred senses*, back to the well of wisdom. The wisdom that we gain from the well is not just the wisdom of the Otherworld, it is the wisdom of the self. It is the *aos dana* who drink from the well; the gifted ones. Within the word dana, we have the word *dán*, a word which we will discuss more throughout this course. It means art, gift, poetry, and destiny. Our *dán* is the soul-gift that we were born to bring into the world, it is our wisdom-art that is recovered during the initiatory process, is kindled within us, to be birthed into the waiting world. As poet David Whyte so aptly shows us:

> *To be human*
> *is to become visible*
> *while carrying*
> *what is hidden*
> *as a gift to others.*

This then is the journey you are about to embark upon. There is no distance to the journey however, only the plunging in to your own depths to recover the gift you were born to be living.

CHAPTER ONE

The Rite of Passage

In "earth-honoring" societies a central aspect of development is the rite of passage. Often this is expressed in the passage of a child to an adult, and all that might entail. It seems appropriate then, to begin the Ovate course with something of a rite of passage to mark the transition from Bard to Ovate; into a deeper experience of and participation in the traditions.

Just as there are three major stages of initiation – the collapse of the old life, the seeking of new vision, and the tending and embodiment of that vision – so too we might speak of the three Druid grades as a similar process. Whereas the Bardic course was setting up the foundations of what a life on the Druid path might look like, the Ovate course lies in the cultivation of that life, and a vision to sustain it. The Druid course will be an engagement in how to integrate this vision into your life.

The rite of passage that we offer here, is a relatively simple one, though hopefully no less potent for it. It does not require anything more from you than your time and a willingness to engage your own inner process of transformation and initiation. The rite centers around a piece of music called *Spirit Vessel*. This is an "entheogenic soundscape" in the tradition of Steve Roach and Byron Metcalf. You might imagine it as literally being the vessel which will carry you from the Bardic work to the Ovate work.

My last words before outlining the process are these: this can be an intense piece of music, which can bring up intense emotions and states of consciousness. Honor your process, but also your limits. Above all be gentle with yourself. If during the course of the work, you feel overwhelmed, I invite you to bring your awareness to your breath, and simply breathe through the difficulty. If you find you need to stop the process at any time, that is perfectly acceptable.

Spirit Vessel

- Set a day (or half day at the least) aside to focus on this practice. When you awake in the morning you may want to meditate if you do not regularly do so, and perhaps spend some time at your altar if you have one. Attend to the cultivation of vision.

- At a suitable time, without distractions, start making a list of all the aspects of your self and your life that are not in service to your Deep Self, or soul. What parts of your self and your life can you shed to attune to the deeper currents of the life of your soul? Use a "soft gaze" and be honest with yourself. You will gain nothing from lying.

- When your list feels complete set up your space so that it is conducive to soul work. I suggest laying down for this part of the process, but if you are more comfortable sitting or standing, go with what feels right. If you have an altar you may want to be present at it. If it is daytime, you might consider closing the curtains or otherwise blocking the light out.

- Get in your space and put Spirit Vessel either into your stereo or play it on your computer. It is about 24 minutes long, so be sure to allow yourself enough time.

- Hold within you those things that you wish to shed, and allow the music to wash over you, and just "ride" its currents to see where it takes you.

- When you hear the call back signal at the end of the second track, come back to the room by slowly starting to move your body, and when you feel ready, open your eyes, sit up, and place your hands on the floor palms down.

- You might want to take some time to reflect and journal on your experience before returning to your day.

- Pay attention to your dreams.

CHAPTER TWO

Awareness Practice 1: The Physical Senses

Throughout this course you will find a series of stopping-places, which I have called *Awareness Practices*. These are practices of becoming mindful of our relationship with nature, with our senses, and the non-ordinary Otherworld. The focus of this course is on the practice, rather than the accompanying readings and writing assignments.

This practice is quite simple, but the experience can be quite profound. How often do we attend to the physical presence of nature? Even when out on the land, many of us have a tendency to become distracted. We find our minds wandering from us, and suddenly we aren't in nature at all! We are back at the office, class, old arguments, or thinking ahead to what we will have for dinner.

The practice, then, is this: spend some time out in nature; as much time as you can give. It doesn't matter particularly *how*. Go for a hike, sit under a tree, wander aimlessly through a park, or go wading in a stream. Attend to the physical presence of nature. You might find it helpful to spend time with each of your physical senses individually.

What do you hear? Spend time just listening to nature, both its sounds and silence. What do you see? Spend time focusing on color, light, shadow, movement, and stillness. What do you smell? Spend time with the smells of nature; smell the flowers, the grass, and the soil. What do you taste? Don't be afraid to get in there! What does the air taste like? If you know of the edible plants in the area, taste them (warning: do not do this unless you are absolutely certain of the plant).

Now bring your awareness back to the whole picture, and just spend some time being mindful and aware of it all, whatever information registers to your senses.

You might also try the following when you have finished: repeat this sensory exercise in a town or city. What do you notice about the way your senses react in both areas. Where do they open up the most? Where do they shut down? Spend as much time with this exercise as you'd like. I invite you to come back to it often, as the course proceeds, and beyond. Spending time with and attuning to the physical presence of nature can reveal just as many treasures to us as speaking with the spirits and attending to the non-ordinary layers of reality.

CHAPTER THREE

Wild Earth, Wild Mind:
The Story of the Soul of Place

Ah, not to be cut off,
not through the slightest partition
shut out from the law of the stars
The inner – what is it?
if not intensified sky,
hurled through with birds and deep
with the winds of homecoming.
- Rainer Maria Rilke

Everything is a story. In the march of progress we have lost our place in the greater story of all things, and so have lost a vital soul-piece. To step out of this story is to risk everything. We have proved this beyond a doubt. The destruction of the environment has coincided with a collective sense of alienation, disenfranchisement, and deracination. Every day in our rationalized insanity we further the destruction and desecration of the earth. Thomas Berry reminds us that "a degraded habitat will produce degraded humans."[1] Healing this degradation of self and world is the task of an emerging era in human history. We must adapt and step back into a relationship of reciprocity with the story of a more-than-human world.

We are undoubtedly a part of this world. We were birthed out of it, and so maintain a bonded relationship with the earth. Modern psychology has been thus far unable to recognize this. However, what more fundamental relationship could exist than the one between a being and its place. Place is the most pervasive of all influences on the psyche. This understanding has been explored in the more accepted domain of environmental psychology, however this discipline largely fails due to its anthropocentric nature of focusing on the use of environment to stimulate human wellness.

The emerging, and far more radical, field of ecopsychology goes steps beyond this. Ecopsychology is a direct reaction to our stepping out of alignment with the story of place and being. Even the word "ecopsychology", as theorist John David points out, comes from ecopsyche-logos: the story of the soul of the home or the story of the home of the soul.[2] It is the study of the human soul in relationship to the soul of nature. As such it recognizes the need for reciprocity between the two, and that because nature has a soul, it has intrinsic value, completely independent of our human need for its resources.

Psychology itself suggests that it is the study of the soul, however it seems to have come a long way from these roots in the modern West. Transpersonal psychology has done a lot to reclaim the spiritual dimension of psychology, however it often tends to over-spiritualize things and holds to the opinion that the only value to physical nature is that it is an expression of spirit. Ecopsychology on the other hand recognizes the spiritual in nature, but also states boldly that the physicality of nature is just as important as the soul of nature. After all, we don't relate to other humans merely for the experience of getting into contact with their soul. We relate to the entirety of their being as it is expressed, both as spiritual and physical. This is especially evident in sexual relationships. This is the relationship being pointed to in the ancient mythological theme of land-as-lover.

Many of the world's indigenous earth-honoring spiritual traditions might be considered primal ecopsychologies, or as Theodore Roszak calls them "stone age psychologies". In the modern study of ecopsychology the traditions of shamanic and animistic people are often looked at for the parallel concepts and practices that it shares in common. This is an important part of the work because it embraces the reclamation of our indigenous soul. Culture is so entwined with the land from which it emerged, that alienation from place is often synonymous with alienation from an authentic relationship to culture.

To be indigenous, one does not have to be rooted in the same land as their ancestors or part of an unbroken native cultural tradition; few in fact still exist which have avoided influences from the modern world. Rather, to be indigenous means to be located in a place, and for that place to inform the way in which you belong to the world. For this reason we might consider an important supporting addition to ecopsychology to be a form of cultural psychology; a practice of reconnection for the displaced and uprooted.

The Celtic spiritual traditions provide such a framework of connection. The Irish word tuatha is a beautiful expression of the inherent ecopsychological leanings that characterize the primal Celtic spirit. Tuatha has a dual meaning; it refers to both the people and the land in a single breath. Tuatha does not just mean the land as the ground below our feet; its connotation is of the land-as-place. This is an important distinction, as it essentially recognizes the soul of the place. It is the place of the people, but as the word suggests, the place and the people are not separate entities; they are one and the same. Such is the intimacy of this relationship that the land is the people and the people are the land.

To talk about the interaction of soul and place, we need to clarify what we mean by "soul" and what we mean by "nature". Depth psychologist and ecotherapist, Bill Plotkin, defines soul as "the vital, mysterious, and wild core of our individual selves, an essence unique to each person, qualities found in layers of the self, much deeper than our personalities."[3] In Jungian psychology the soul is understood to be the Self, which is independent of the ego. This is beautifully articulated in a poem by the early 20th century Spanish poet, Jiménez:

> I am not I.
> I am this one
> Walking beside me whom I do not see,
> Whom at times I manage to visit,
> And whom at other times I forget;
> The one who remains silent when I talk,
> The one who forgives, sweet, when I hate,
> The one who takes a walk where I am not,
> The one who will remain standing when I die.
> (translated by Robert Bly)

In many ancient cultures the soul is often related to the air or breath. This sentiment survives in the Irish language, in the connection between the words *anam* (soul) and *anáil* (breath). In Latin, another Indo-European language (which is also the "mother language" of Irish), the connection is even more closely expressed, and anima is the word for both soul and breath. Breath is air, and this shatters the common Western assertion that the soul is trapped within the body and in need of liberation. On the contrary the soul is something we intimately engage in each moment, it is both all around us and infusing our being with life (which is another meaning of the Irish word anam). As poet-philosopher John O'Donohue writes, "The body is your clay home, your only home in the universe. The body is in the soul; this recognition confers a sacred and mystical dignity on the body."[4]

Inherent in this understanding is the claim that even the individual soul, or Self, participates in a much wider relationship with the world. It is as pervasive as the air we breathe. The soul extends beyond our limited notions of the egoic-self, and engages and relates with all that it comes into contact with. In this understanding, soul is hardly limited to the human soul. It touches and infuses everything with story. There is nothing that does not participate in this dialogue. This is the foundation of animistic thought; there is soul in everything and nature is the most elegant expression of soul as matter.

This of course still leaves us grasping with the question of what nature is. It might seem obvious at first, but upon closer examination becomes as elusive in defining as the evershifting Otherworld of the Celtic world. In many ways it defies categorization and definitions because it so absolutely fundamental and pervasive of our human experience.

Nature might be thought of as the physical and sensual world which retains the integrity of its core wildness. Because humans are a part of nature, this does not necessarily mean that nature is everything divorced from the impacts of human activity. We might say that nature is the sensuous places in which soul dwells. Rather than defining nature as everything Other than human, we can make the leap to include ourselves within this spectrum. But neither is nature just the phenomenal world; it is also the spiritual, cultural, and psychological dimensions contained therein. In this understanding nature and soul are one, and neither is raised in importance above the other. A tree is just as much a soul as it is a collection of wood cells and chlorophyll. Neither experience of the tree is more primary or valuable than the other because they are essentially the same experience to begin with.

This stands in direct contrast to attempts to over-spiritualize nature. Sometimes it is spiritual enough to just stand and feel the wind through your hair, the icy winter rain across your face, or listen to the gushing of a stream under the diverse and brilliant color of autumn leaves. Hidden within this sensual experience of nature is exactly where we meet the storied presence of soul.

The soul of place is an invisible presence that permeates the land. It is the Land behind the land, just as our own soul if the Self behind the self, "walking beside me whom I do not see". One has only to be touched by the beauty of the natural world to know this power; a cloud-covered mountain peak, the bright sun shining yellow-green through a canopy of forest leaves, the flight of geese reflected in the clear blue water of a dark lake. The soul of place reveals itself in the pure and authentic presence that nature holds herself in.

When we cease to experience the presence of the world, we lose our own sense of presence, and further alienate ourselves from nature and soul. However if we are willing to join in this dynamic dance of nature, our own sense of soulful presence becomes enlivened within us. This sort of dialogue between nature and soul came to expression in a poem of mine:

PRESENCE

Something about
the way
mountains and trees
dance with the shapes
of clouds;
the symphonic echo
of stillness against the
steady relaxed drifting
and gentle waving that's
beckoned by wind.
Beneath it the lake
answers back with
portraits of clarity
wrapped in the ripples
of its own interpretation.

Presence is the
spontaneous joining in
of our own
surprised voices.

The interaction between the soul of place and the human community is of prime importance in shamanic cultures. There is much debate about whether or not Celtic culture was a "shamanic" one. Much of this debate hinges on the way in which we define shamanism. Most scholars tend to focus on it as what Mircea Eliade called an "archaic technique of ecstasy", and focus on the shaman's ability to heal and travel to the spirit realm. This however ignores the most important function of the shaman: that of mediator between the human community and nature, or the soul of place.

If we contemplate the shaman from this perspective, we can begin to understand that the shamans were the first ecopsychologists. Their ability to heal was grounded in the continued reciprocity between the human and natural communities. There was a recognition that disease and illnesses were largely a product of an imbalance in this more primal relationship. David Abram articulates this well in an interview, The Ecology of Magic:

If the magician was not simultaneously doing this work of offering prayers and praises and ritual gestures to the other animals and to the powers of the earth and the sky, then he might heal someone in the community and someone else would fall sick, and then he would heal that other person, and someone else would fall sick. The source of the illness is often perceived as an imbalance within the person, but it is actually in the relation between the human village and the land that supports it, the land that yields up its food, its animals for skins for clothing, and its plants for food and medicine. Humans take so much from the land, and the magician's task is to make sure that we humans always return something to the land so that there is a two-way flow, that the boundary between us – the human culture and the rest of nature – stays a porous boundary.[5]

It is this role which marks the druid of Celtic culture as a shamanic figure and an ancient expression of ecopsychology. Druids, though they had a wide role to play in society – including everything from historians to judges to healers, diviners, and spiritual counselors –might be summed up best as keepers of memory and reciprocity between the tribe and the land. They were threshold people who through their cultivated skills mediated this relationship. Though the druids may have played a central role in Celtic society, it is worth noting that the ordinary people of the community also participated in the same worldview and were responsible for their own personal relationship with the gods and the land.

As historians, storytellers, and genealogists, the druids played the role of tribal memory keepers. This keeping of memory was also an important part of their role as cultivators of reciprocity. An early Irish text, the Senchus Mór, asks the question, "What is the preserving shrine?" It replies to itself, "Not hard: it is memory and what is preserved in it." Seeking depth and clarification, it asks the question again, "What is the preserving shrine? Not hard: it is nature and what is preserved in it". The preserving shrine is the memory of the land. The understanding that the land has a memory is radical to the modern world, but pervasive to ancient thought. This is essentially an articulation of the soul of place.

The dinnseanchas, the place-name stories of Ireland, are a perfect example of the interplay of memory and land. Each place has its name and the story of how that name came to be associated with that place. Although many of the surviving dinnseanchas are medieval fabrications, there are authentic stories mixed within and the survival of the tradition speaks to the Celtic propensity to situate themselves in a storied and enlivened world.

This sort of practice is by no means limited to the Celtic people. The Apache tribes of North America also have a strong tradition of place oriented stories. Similarly the Aboriginal people of Australia have the tradition of the songlines. In fact the dinnseanchas might be thought of as the "Celtic songlines" in some respects. The dinnseanchas are an expression of the Celtic dreamtime, the mytho-poetic history of the relationship between people, the gods, and the land. In many such place-name story traditions, including the songlines of Australia, it is in the retelling of the stories the place is renewed and recreated. This is much like the ritual re-enactment of the cosmogony of a people, which is evident in most native cultures around the world. It had a firm presence in the Celtic world as well at each of the four seasonal festivals. One might speculate that the dinnseanchas served a similar purpose. By telling these stories we participate in this mytho-poetic process of creation and thus renew the land and revitalize our relationship to it.

Oral cultures recognize, far more so than our written and alphabetic culture, the power of words. For oral cultures, language was a matter of the body and senses, rather than the disembodied abstract use of written language that our culture is accustomed to. The name of something was not just a series of self-reflective human symbols, but a deep and embodied experience of the thing itself. In a sense, the name of something was the thing, as well as a recognition of its enlivened nature. This theme is powerfully explored in David Abram's book, The Spell of the Sensuous: Language and Perception in a More-Than-Human World.

Storytelling, specifically in the context of myth, is about creating a threshold. Myths and stories take us to a place that is not quite fact, not quite fiction – it is someplace between these two. It is a liminal place from which we can access the Otherworld which is the indefinable, elusive, and shapeshifting interiority of place and individual; the place, to use Theodore Roszak's term, "where psyche meets Gaia". The dinnseanchas provide an excellent medium for this dialogue because they deal directly in the subject matter of place. The dinnseanchas provide this threshold – between memory and nature, fact and fiction, human and other – and thus allow us to navigate and mediate the energy of reciprocity across the boundaries.

A specific story from the dinnseanchas, dealing with the creation and naming of the Boyne River in Ireland, captures this sense well. In this story, the goddess Boann is married to Nechtan, who is the protector of a sacred well in the realm of his sidhe. Only Nechtan and his three cupbearers were able to approach the well. Boann, however, attempts to do this. Interestingly she walks around the well counterclockwise. The waters from the well rise up, and injure her, taking one of her eyes, a leg, and an arm. The waters then chase her to the place of the Boyne River's mouth, where she is "killed" and becomes the river.

Within this story we engage in the reality of the land as threshold. The injuries Boann sustains are a common motif in several stories. One of those stories is the Second Battle of Magh Tuireadh, in which Lugh takes on the "crane posture" of standing on one leg, with one eye closed, and one hand behind his back. There seems to be a threshold significance to this posture, in that it represents having one foot in both worlds. One might be able to view these injuries purely as a punishment for her violations of a taboo, however it seems obvious that something deeper is happening here. The well in question is the well of wisdom after all, and it is those waters which were released into the world. This sort of relationship with the land after all, with the sources of wisdom, is not without risk; through it we are transformed, and like Boann become threshold people, with our senses enmeshed deep within both nature and soul.

The dinnseanchas are in this way an entwining of nature and memory. Memory, and the cultivation of memory, was an important aspect of druidic training. This was for several reasons, not least of which was that in an oral culture, the extent of the memory determines the extent to which the traditions endure. However as memory-keepers – poets, historians, storytellers, genealogists, lore and tradition bearers –this meant more than the simple passing on of information. By holding the memory of all they did, they essentially were able to remind the ordinary people of the tribe who they were, both within the human world, as well as citizens of a more-than-human world.

The druid was precisely that person who had gone to the well of wisdom, like Boann, drank from its secret waters, and thus stood on the threshold between this world and the Other, mediating between the two. It should come as no surprise then to find that there is a possible etymological connection between the word druid and the Sanskrit word *duir*, which also gives us the English word "door". The druids acted as hallowed representatives of the Earth Mother, and served the people as a doorway, a point of entry, into the sacred world.

If nature is the sensuous places in which soul dwells, then it is essentially that which connects us to the sacred, and fosters our relationship to the sacred world. This relationship to the sacred is as much an aspect of druidism, shamanism, and ecopsychology as the relationship of reciprocity to the phenomenal world of the senses. In fact, the two are co-arising, and one cannot exist without the other. To alienate ourselves from nature is to alienate ourselves from soul, from the sacred, and thus to become a mirror solely of the human world. Just as David Abram reminds us, "We are human only in contact and conviviality with what is not human. Only in reciprocity with what is Other do we begin to heal ourselves."[6] Otherwise we are like the written word, divorced and disembodied from the sensual world.

This connection to the sacred is as vital as air and water to our continued survival. The sacred facilitates the expansive relationship between humans and the world. It is the sacred which drives us towards this relationship because through it we recognize our kinship with all the soulful and animated world. Gary Snyder writes that "Sacred refers to that which helps take us out of our little selves into the larger self of the whole universe."[7] Earth-honoring cultures remember this well, and life is oriented to the cultivation of this relationship, and thus to the movement from the "little self" into the "larger self" of the soul.

We can see this clearly in the Celtic world. There is perhaps no better evidence for this than the Carmina Gadelica, a compilation of prayers, charms, and invocations from the Scottish Gaelic world. Although the compilation is Scottish, there are similar prayers from Ireland and it would be far from irrational speculation to suggest that the tradition thrived there as well. Most of these prayers had to do with the ordinary. They concerned things like sowing seeds, going to sleep, waking from the night, lighting the hearth fire or smooring it in the evening. They were simple prayers, filled with a sense and presence of the sacred, which were recited throughout the day to keep one "in contact and conviviality" with the more-than-human. As evidenced by the compilation, this practice endured strongly in rural places even into the 19th and early 20th century.

When our world is enlivened by the sacred, even the so called "ordinary" becomes a profound expression of beauty. There is no such "thing" as the sacred, because all things are sacred. Instead it is more of an experience, a relationship, a way of seeing the world. In this way of seeing all things are enlivened, and so move away from the objective world of "things" and come to rest and belong in the subjective world of "beings". Because stories connect us with the sacred, and bring us into experiential relationship to it, they are a potent bridge which crosses the perceptual gap between the sacred and the ordinary.

In losing our own story in relation to the sacred world we have lost our bridge. That is to say that we have come to believe the illusion that there is a gap. This gap is the same one which leaves us stranded on one side and the more-than-human on the other side. It sanctions the realm of nature and the realm of soul to their separate sides of experience, leaving us bereft of their true unity. The illusion of the gap is one that leads us to need phrases like "human-nature relationship" which stresses separation and division. In truth though, this illusion becomes obvious as soon as we stop trying to live with nature, and begin living as nature, as members of a community of subjective beings.

To do this we need to reclaim our place in the story, which is to say that we need to be placed in a landscape and a spiritscape that is imbued with story, with consciousness, and enlivened by soul. In the presence of story there is the potential for soul-encounter – in ourselves, in others, in the land, and the more-than-human world. In many respects story and soul are one, because they are the subjective narrative of Self.

This of course raises the question of the story of the land. After all, don't we give and imbue the land with story? We most certainly do, but this is at best only a half truth. We can flip that very question around and point it just as effectively at ourselves. Doesn't the land give and imbue us with story? What story would humans have without the land, without the more-than-human world? We would have no story at all. The human story does not cause and create the story of the land. They co-arise from within because they are both essentially the same story. There is only the One Story. No matter whether we hear it through the wind in the trees, the lapping of the ocean at the shore, the slow rising of mountains from the ground, the hooting of owls in the night, the cawing of ravens, the stags bellowing, or the voices of humans telling tales around the hearth. It is all one story of the soulful presence of the world.

We stand at a junction in history. The old human story is collapsing – revealing itself for its own myopic nature – and the institutions that once held and reinforced it are collapsing with it. The new story that is emerging is the one which calls us into creative kinship with the presence of the world. The druids of old practiced in their *neimheadh*, their nemetons, or forest-shrines. Returning to the neimheadh can be a profound metaphor for our return to the life-affirming story that we are now being called to surrender to. It is perhaps no accident that enfolded within this word is another word: neimhe. Heaven. Whether there are actual etymological roots between the two, or if it is just another note within the life-dream to startle us awake, ultimately does not matter. It is an invitation to sit in presence with a very simple fact: heaven has never been far; it is waiting patiently for our return to the wild and soulful earth.

Endnotes

1. Louv, Richard. "New world beyond the levees". The San Diego Union-Tribune. 4 October, 2005. 18 April, 2006.
http://www.signonsandiego.com/uniontrib/20051004/news_lz1e4louv.html

2. Swift, Jed. "An Overview of Ecopsychology". PSYT351e Ecopsychology. Naropa University, Boulder, Colorado. September 2005.

3. Plotkin, Bill. *Soulcraft: Crossing into the Mysteries of Nature and Psyche*. New World Library: Novato, 2003. p. 25

4. O' Donohue, John. *Anam C.ara: Spiritual Wisdom from the Celtic World*. Bantam Books: London, 1997. p. 17

5. London, Scott. "The Ecology of Magic: An Interview with David Abram". Scott London. 2006. 18 April, 2006. http://www.scottlondon.com/interviews/abram.html

6. Abram, David. *The Spell of the Sensuous*. Vintage Books: New York, 1996. p. 22

7. Snyder, Gary. *Good Wild Sacred*. Five Seasons Press: Herefore, England, 1984. p. 26.

Further Reading
FOR WILD EARTH, WILD MIND

Cowan, Tom. *Yearning for the Wind: Celtic Reflections on Nature and the Soul*. Novato, California: New World Library, 2003.

Metzner Ph.D., Ralph. *Green Psychology: Transforming Our Relationship to the Earth*. Rochester, Vermont: Park Street Press, 1999.

Monaghan, Patricia. *The Red-Haired Girl from the Bog: The Landscape of Celtic Myth and Spirit*. Novato, California: New World Library, 2003.

Plotkin, Bill. *Soulcraft: Crossing into the Mysteries of Nature and Psyche*. Novato, California: New World Library, 2003.

Roszak, Theodore. *The Voice of the Earth: An Exploration of Ecopsychology*. Grand Rapids, Missouri: Phanes Press, 1992.

Roszak, Theodore; Gomes, Mary E.; Kanner Allen D. (editors). *Ecopsychology: Restoring the Earth, Healing the Mind*. San Francisco, California: Sierra Club Books, 1995.

CHAPTER FOUR

The Way of the Anam Cara:
Nature and Belonging

Life is a pilgrimage; we walk this ancient soil where our ancestors have also stepped, and we are confronted with the chance to listen deeply to the wisdom in our blood and in the bones of the earth. This wisdom speaks of our ancient bonds and connections. It tells us that although we often feel utterly lost and alone, we truly are not. We are all part of something that lies just below the surface of the waters of appearance.

In the primal traditions of Ireland, there exists a custom of having an *anam cara*, or "soul friend". In Celtic Christianity, this is the person who will be there to comfort a dying person and guide the passage of their soul. It is often used in a much more general sense however, as simply a co-walker in our spiritual life who's soul touches our own. In the pain of our spiritual journeys, our pilgrimage through life, the anam cara is the one who we can unburden ourselves to. It is a relationship with a person that allows an opening and dynamic exchange of soul between friends.

The anam cara is not exclusive to human beings however. Celtic consciousness is one of animistic perception, and so all the world is imbued with a luminous divine energy, sometimes spoken of as the Earth Mother. Each tree, river, stone, and mountain has its own in-dwelling spirit and its own stories to tell. The spirit of these things can also act as anam cara. There are traditions of *cranncainte* and *tonncainte*, literally meaning, "speaking with the trees" and "speaking with the waves", where a person is able to make contact with nature to heal wounds and gain wisdom. Whether tree, ocean, or simply the soil beneath our feet, the Earth takes our spiritual and emotional waste and transforms it, just as animal waste becomes fertilizer for new vegetation.

Beneath all of this though, is perhaps an even more important anam cara: the Earth Mother, or divinity itself. This energy is the essence of our great belonging. The Celtic view of the cosmos is highly inclusive and within it all things are perceived as sacred, just as all things are held within the sheltering spirit of divinity. There are no boundaries that state that supposed dualities are in contradiction, or that one aspect of life is more important than another. Farming, spirituality, politics, and family life are all woven into one, because fundamentally they all deal with the same underlying reality.

As a society we have largely forgotten this reality. We have forgotten our luminous bonds with one another and to the universe. With the loss of these bonds, we have experienced the loss of our ability to perceive the world as sacred. We have drawn lines between what is sacred and what is mundane, where the boundaries occur between heaven and earth, and we have placed these things in opposition to one another. These boundaries no longer meet, and are no longer as permeable as they once were.

I call this the wounded soul. It is noted in some way or another in many of the world's wisdom traditions, as well as in our evolving understanding of the eco-psychological relationship between human and nature. The wound is characterized through many of the ailments we find in the modern world; a feeling of alienation, despair, being spiritually and culturally disenfranchised, and bereft of any sense of belonging or home. There is a deep yearning within our hearts to reclaim some lost portion of ourselves, which often is played out in those movements that urge us to return to some primal state of well being. However, healing does not lie in the past, but rather here in our daily lives, our relationship to the universe, and to each other. It is up to us to initiate this process of healing and the befriending of the universe.

Longing, an important and powerful force in the Celtic traditions, is also a practice that we can cultivate to help facilitate this healing. Longing is what sent Celtic Christian seekers out into nature to search alone for God in what is called the Green Martyrdom. Longing and belonging are profoundly linked, and it is the belonging of God that these mystics were looking for. By allowing themselves to be absorbed into nature, they were giving themselves to the untamed wilderness of the soul, and thus transcending ego. They were accepting the universe as friend, as anam cara. The bridge between our alienation from, and friendship to the universe, is longing. Longing bridges the gap between the darkness of our suffering and loneliness with the intimacy of friendship and community. When we can befriend our world we are taking a step back into a relationship with the reality of the spirit, rather than the reality of the ego. This is a way of softening the edges of ourselves, making us vulnerable and open to the shaping powers of the universe.

In this sense friendship is perhaps one of the most important things that could be cultivated in one's life. Finding an anam cara is a practice of healing the wounded soul. Whether this means finding a person to whom you can share your soul, engaging with nature and the spirit of place, or rekindling our ancient bonds with the Spirit of Life, it is a way of orienting ourselves to a life of sacred perception and aligning to the holy reality of the universe. By practicing the ancient tradition of befriending the universe, we can begin to heal many of the wounds that our souls have incurred. In the words of John O'Donohue, author of *Anam Cara: A Book of Celtic Wisdom*, "When you are blessed with an anam cara, the Irish believe, you have arrived at that most sacred place: home." The Celts have always been a wandering people, and home is not any physical location but rather the Otherworld that exists between the mists. And so the tradition of the anam cara is a doorway or threshold that helps to orient us to the Otherworld, where the boundaries between apparent opposites are dissolved. We are then plunged into the healing springs where spirit and nature meet, and we regain our sacred senses.

Further Reading
FOR THE WAY OF THE ANAM CARA

O'Donohue, John. *Anam Cara: Spiritual Wisdom from the Celtic World. London, Great Britain: Bantam Books, 1997.*

O'Donohue, John. *Eternal Echoes: Celtic Reflections on Our Yearning to Belong.* New York, New York: HarperCollins, 1999.

O'Donohue, John. *Divine Beauty: The Invisible Embrace.* London, Great Britain: Bantam Books, 2003.

Note that these may appear with alternative titles depending on the country in which they were published. For example *Divine Beauty* is simply called *Beauty* if you purchase it from a publisher in the United States.

CHAPTER FIVE

Awareness Practice II: Place-Bonding

1. Go out into the green world of nature; the wilder the better. If the only place you can get away to is a local park, the backyard, or even just a house plant, then that is fine. Whatever is available will work.

2. Find a place that you are drawn to, which is comfortable enough to spend a bit of time in. It might be a particular tree, a stone, beside a stream, a clearing in a forest, you're favorite corner of the yard, or your beloved venus fly trap.

3. Make yourself comfortable and just take some time to arrive. Tune in to your physical senses. As the saying goes, "notice what you notice".

4. Begin by becoming aware of yourself as being the "watcher" of the place. Now shift your perception, and become aware of yourself as the "watched". Continue shifting back and forth between these, noticing what you notice.

5. Next, bring your attention to the physical presence of your place. Sit with this for a while.

6. Now imagine for a moment that what you are feeling as the physical presence of the place is also the spiritual presence of the place. Sit with this for a while.

7. Cycle between this experience of the physical and spiritual presence of place. Notice what you notice.

8. Now become aware of yourself as being *part* of this place, as much as the trees, the plants, the streams, the house cats, etc. What is it like to participate in the experience of place?

Some questions to spend some time with after this exercise:

- *While doing this exercise, did I experience something that I would consider sacred?*
- *Of the two experiences of place; the physical and the "spiritual", which one did you perceive as the soul of place?*
- *This exercise asks you to contemplate a fundamental gap between nature and soul. What are the problems posed by perceiving the physical and spiritual as a duality?*

Optional: Try the above exercise in an urban setting. What do you notice?

CHAPTER SIX

Truth and Sovereignty:
Sacred Warriorship in the Celtic Traditions

It is popular today to talk of being a "spiritual warrior". What I am about to describe has little, if anything, to do with many of the romantic "New Age" notions of warriorship (which are often, or it seems to me, simply a stroking of the ego). It also has nothing to do with the cultivation of anger, brute strength, and unbalanced masculine archetypes of aggression. That said, it has a great deal to do with Truth and Sovereignty.

Let us begin by examining Truth in the Celtic tradition. I capitalize the word *Truth* for a specific reason. I am not referring here to the concept of honesty or the correlation of facts. As Tom Cowan points out in *Yearning for the Wind: Celtic Reflections on Nature and the Soul*, "None of these is deep enough or eternal enough. Truth...is a relationship with life, a relationship known deep in the soul that balances our personal lives with the Great Life Itself."[1] Truth as relationship is a radical concept to the current prevailing worldview. It would not, however, be news to many ancient cultures. Similar in scope perhaps to the Navajo concept of Beauty, and the Chinese notion of the Tao (which is often translated to simply mean "the Way"), Truth in the Celtic tradition would not be so strange an idea to other earth-centered people. It is about the fundamental unity and balance of all things within a greater whole. As author Greywind defines it in his book, *The Voice Within the Wind*, Truth is "a measurement of the degree of which a thing is rightly integrated with the underlying unity of all things." When we live our lives in Truth, we are living our lives in harmony with the world and with our soul.

Truth is important to the integrity of the world. Truth, in fact, is not *just* a measurement to how integrated a thing or person is with the Soul of Life, it is the force that binds all things together. This is evidenced by several strands of Celtic thought. On the one hand we have the story of Cormac mac Art and his Cup of Truth. When a lie was spoken over this cup, it shattered. It took three truths to restore the cup to wholeness. We see this story mirrored in a Celtic oath which proclaims, "May the sea rise up to swallow me, the earth open up to swallow me, and the sky fall upon my head if I be forsworn." The cosmos itself could be understood to be a macrocosm of Cormac's Cup of Truth, and it is by cultivating right relationship to the world that it is bound together, both within and without.

We also have accounts of advice from Druids and wise kings to future rulers on the importance of the "truth of the ruler". As we have studied in *An Audacht Morainn*, or the Testament of Morann, truth played an important part of the rule of a king. It was through the truth of the king that the fitness of things was maintained, that the land remained fertile, and that the people flourished. The king's truth kept the cosmos in order.

The so-called "high kingship" in Ireland was not much of a social position. It was a ritual position, and could perhaps be more accurately called the "sacral kingship". It is interesting to note that despite the stress of kings in Celtic society, there is no word for coronation. The word in Irish is *bainís rí*, and means "marriage of the king". This refers to a ritual marriage between the king and the goddess of the land; the goddess of sovereignty. For the king of Tara this would probably be under the guise of the goddess Maeve, who I will discuss shortly.

This does not however apply only to kings in the common sense of the word, as a person who rules over others. In fact, perhaps it applies even more to the sense of the king as one who rules him or herself. Central to the Celtic way of being in the world is *laochra*. Laochas in modern Irish means "heroism" or "valour". Each person in Celtic society was the hero, but also the king, of their own life. In terms of the sacred warriorship this means that each person is responsible for stepping into alignment with sovereignty, and with Truth. This comes surprisingly close to the Shambhala warriorship of the Tibetan tradition with concepts such as the universal monarch. From a mystical perspective Laochas is sacred warriorship.

When St. Patrick asked one of the Fianna (a band of warriors-outcasts who protected Ireland) who had returned from the Otherworld after the coming of Christianity, what sustained the warriors before the gospels, he answered, "The truth in our hearts, the strength in our hands, and the promise on our lips."[2] We get the sense from this that the Fianna were not aggressive brutes living off the thrills of violence. Something deeper served as the enlivening principle to their lives. It may be important to note that all of the stories about the Fianna take place in the wilds of nature; that nature was the world in which they lived, fought, and died.

Nature and communion with the land has a lot to do with truth, sovereignty, and the sacred warriorship. As we have seen, the kings ability to rule is dependent on his marriage to the goddess of the land. Just so, our ability to "rule our lives" so to speak, is dependent on an active and engaged relationship with the powers of nature and the earth. The story of the Irish epic of *Táin Bo Cuailgne*, or the Cattle Raid of Cooley gives us some instructions as to how to honor this relationship.

One of the main characters of the story is the goddess and queen, Medb. Medb is the goddess associated with the Hill of Tara, and is named the intoxicating one. It is she that gives her name to the sacred drink of Mead. As the goddess of the land, it is not surprising then to find that she has rules for those who would "be her husband". It is Medb that demands our Truth. Tom Cowan calls these Queen Maeve's Rules for Soul Making. He must be without fear, without jealousy, and without stinginess.

Fearlessness does not mean we are absent of fear. As Chogyam Trungpa explains in his book, *Shambhala: The Sacred Path of the Warrior*, fearlessness has more to do with a willingness to go *into* what we fear. It is a willingness to always live in alignment with our Truth no matter the cost. Sometimes Truth can be a very painful road in life. Sometimes living in our Truth requires us to sacrifice something, to go to frightening places in our psyche and in the world. Sometimes it also means turning our backs on those things, places, and people with which we have harmful relationships with that for whatever reason cannot be healed at the time. Often living in Truth requires that we move into our pain. It takes great courage to do these things, as well as the cultivation of fearlessness and a gentleness of spirit. Fearlessness is not hard, but rather it is very soft and tender. If we move into these things with a hard mind we will likely end up doing damage where we meant to heal. For that reason compassion for self and others is the twin sister of fearlessness.

Medb also requires that we be without jealousy, for as she says in the Táin, "I am never with one man without another waiting in his shadow." Jealousy is the desire to possess what another has, and that we are without. As such it comes from a place of being unable to recognize our interconnectedness; that what another has, we also have. It comes from a place of desire rather than longing. Desire is a need of the ego, and as the Buddhists teach so aptly is a root cause of suffering. Longing on the other hand is rooted in the needs of the soul, and it brings us together in recognition of our interconnectedness. It creates beauty.

It is difficult to talk about being free from jealousy without stepping into the muck and mire of preachy moralization. That is surely not the point of Medb's statements, and most definitely not the point of mine. Although she certainly does paint a particular portrait of a moral code, it should not be seen as a way of making yourself or others guilty about our human shortcomings. We have all been jealous because it is a human emotion and we are all human. The way of the warrior is not so much about *not* feeling particular things, but in seeing them for what they are, and slowly and gently, to move ourselves in a direction that is more in line with the longings of the soul than the desires of the ego.

The final rule that Medb has for us is to be "without stinginess". I see this as almost a reaction to jealousy. If we are without jealousy it is easy to be without stinginess. We become stingy when we over identify with the ego, and believe that by giving something away we are giving away our own vitality. But our life is not hidden in our possessions. This is the great mistake of consumerism. To believe that what we can own and possess will ultimately make us better and fulfill our longings. What we can possess however, always falls short, and soon becomes obsolete. The cycle begins all over again, as we accumulate more and more.

The scene in the *Táin* which follows Medb's listing of her rules may appear greatly ironic in all of this. Medb and her husband have an argument about who is actually the sovereign ruler of their realm, Connaught in the West of Ireland. To settle the dispute, their possessions are paraded out before them to be compared. Ailell wins because he possesses the white bull of Connaught, and so the *Táin* begins, and Medb tries to steal the brown bull of Cooley in order to maintain her position as queen. Cattle of course were the measure of wealth in ancient Irish society. The irony of this should serve as hint that something deeper may be taking place in this story than what appears on the outside.

To be without stinginess is to be generous. Generosity and prosperity in the Celtic traditions have always been symbolic of the land and the goddess of the land. Perhaps this is the reason why the Celts threw so many valuable possessions into rivers, lakes, and bogs. It was in the giving away of wealth to the land that the reciprocity between the human community and the spirits of place was maintained; that the relationship between soul and nature was nourished and sustained. To give away freely in the spirit of generosity is to acknowledge that our vitality is nourished not by the possessive nature of the ego, but in the nourishment of the longings of the soul.

Celtic warriorship is about stepping into right relationship with the world by means of working with the longing of the soul, and being steadfast in that work. It is also deeply rooted in the maintenance of our relationship with the earth. A goddess gives us these instructions and our "marriage", our union with her, is dependent upon our ability to live in Truth. But the way of the warrior is a gentle path, and it is easy to lose our way on it. It is why in the Shambhala tradition, warrior training is synonymous with meditation training. They are mirrors of each other. In meditation it is also easy to forget why we are sitting, and to lose our mindfulness. In this tradition of meditation when we catch ourselves thinking, we simply label those thoughts "thinking" without making a judgement on them, and then return our attention to the breath. The same holds true, in its own way, for the path of warriorship.

Endnotes

1. Cowan, Tom. *Yearning for the Wind: Celtic Reflections on Nature and the Soul.* Novato, California: New World Library, 2003. p. 79.

2. Cowan, p. 83.

Further Reading
FOR TRUTH AND SOVEREIGNTY

Chödron, Pema. *The Places That Scare You: A Guide to Fearlessness*. Boston, Massachusetts: Shambhala Publications, 2001.

Perks, John Riley. *The Mahasiddha and His Idiot Servant*. Putney, Vermont: Crazy Heart Publishers, 2004.

Trungpa, Chögyam. *Shambhala: The Sacred Path of the Warrior*. Boston, Massachusetts: Shambhala Publications, 1984.

CHAPTER SEVEN

Weaving the Soul:
Living in Alignment with Dán

Knowing that it takes only
that one, terrible
word to make the circle complete,

revelation must be terrible
knowing you can
never hide your voice again.[1]
- David Whyte, **Revelation Must Be Terrible,** *Fire in the Earth*

I am fascinated by words and language. Specifically I am fascinated by the weaving of associations and hidden meanings that abound in the connections between words. It is as if all language is a whole, a great weaving of symbolism and meaning, which we cannot always see in all its form. It is like a land covered in thick mist. We can often only see the faint makings of coherence. However in the Celtic tradition, it is within the mist that we are ushered into the Otherworld, and so it is through this misty weaving of language that we are ushered into the power *behind* the words.

There are three words in particular that are of interest to us here: *Dana, dán,* and *bradán.* Dana is a complicated word. It comes from the name of a tribal mother goddess who is often referred to as Danu. The word Dana can be traced back to the Danube River, the area around which the Celtic people emerged. The Indo-European root *da* means "flowing" or "to flow". Similarly the root *danu* which is derived from the prefix *da* means "river". Dana or Danu thus has many associations with waters and the flowing motion of rivers. This makes it a particularly appropriate word to illustrate a "flowing" energy which can be seen in the sense of a soul-nurturing presence, finding its origin within the Earth Mother. However it is energy that can also manifest as the *Cailleach* (kyle-yuck), a goddess figure of destruction and initiatory force. It holds the power of creation and destruction, of life, death, and rebirth, bringing us into contact with our deeper self. It is this initiatory energy than can awaken us to a deeper relationship with the world and our soul.

As the tribal mother goddess Dana can be seen to have been imbued with the energy of the land, the Earth Mother, herself. In most native cultures, the earth is seen as being a woman. This is no less true in Ireland, where the island itself is seen as a goddess, often referred to as a triple goddess Eiru, Banba, and Fotla, from which its name in the Irish language, Éire, is derived. The "flowing" energy, illustrated through the tribal mother, Danu, comes from the land, but it also *is* the land, the Earth Mother, whose hills and mountains are her breasts, and caves her wombs, and all of nature her children.

The third aspect of the Earth Mother's "flowing energy" rests in the idea of earth-spirits and is similar to the kami of Shinto tradition. Patricia Monaghan, in her book *The Red-Haired Girl from the Bog*, describes the kami as such:

> *It describes these moments and places and myth and beings in which divine presence makes itself felt. The blossoming of cherry trees, a sharp outcropping of rock, the sun bursting through clouds: these are kami because they remind us of the order – the divinity – into which we are born. In Ireland, similarly, the goddess is experienced as a hierophany, a breaking through, of divine power into human consciousness, with specific natural settings and moments as the medium of communication.*[2]

This idea also relates to the faery people of Ireland, who are known as the Tuatha Dé Danann (the People of Dán or the People of Danu). One might describe such events, people, or places as being "faery" (although the faeries are quite often experienced as a spirit-people). It would also be appropriate to describe the gods and goddesses of the Irish tradition in this way, who are also said to be Dé Danann, and who were never anthropomorphized like the Greek or Roman gods, but who were more akin to Patricia Monaghan's description of the kami.

Dán is a word which obviously bears a connection to Danu. In fact the name Tuatha Dé Danann is likely a reference to dán, rather than the more common translation, "Children of Danu" or even "People of Danu". The Tuatha Dé Danann were called the *Aois Dana* or "Gifted Ones". It is this gift, or art, which the word dán is pointing towards.

Dán has a whole host of meanings, all of which form a web of deeper symbolism. It can not only mean a gift, but also poetry, art, fate, and destiny. Poet David Whyte, advises us to:

> *Hold to your own truth*
> *at the center of the image*
> *you were born with.*[3]

It is through the crisis of initiation that we encounter our dán, and an opportunity to embody it in the world. During initiation, our ego disintegrates, opening a doorway to the soul, allowing us to form a deeper relationship with this hidden dimension of the self. It is a form of spiritual death which will eventually lead us to rebirth. Our dán dwells in the soul, and during this encounter, we can learn a deeper story than the one which has just died. This is the story we were meant to be living. It is, as another meaning of the word suggests, our destiny. If we are truly living in the current of our dán, we are living our lives, as an unfolding of our authentic self.

The third word in this weave is *bradán*, an Irish word which means salmon. The salmon is a fish of wisdom and figures in as an important animal in Irish mythology. When Cormac MacArt travels to the Otherworldly realm of Manannan MacLir, he sees a pool, which he is told is called the "Pool of Wisdom". From this pool there are five streams which represent the five physical senses through which we perceive our world. The pool itself contains five salmon, and is surrounded by nine hazel trees, which drop their nuts into the water, to be eaten by the salmon. Manannan tells Cormac that everyone drinks from the five streams, but that only poets and gifted ones, the *Aios Dana*, drink from both the streams and the pool.

There is another meaning to the word bradán though. It can also mean the life principle or energy of a person. Life principle, in my understanding, is what a person draws their essential sustenance from, which enlivens them and gives purpose and meaning to their life. These two meanings of the word suggest to us that the most appropriate place to draw our sustenance from is wisdom; from the salmon and the pool.

I would suggest that from the connection between bradán and dán that this is the place to draw our wisdom and sustenance from, the place to go deep within and find our dán. Stepping into the flow of energy from the Earth Mother, as the tribal mother, Danu, illustrates, involves a process of aligning our bradán with our dán; of drawing our essential energy and power from that story we were born to live, the gift we were born to embody. When we can learn to do this we can become agents of this transformative and healing energy.

Dán arises from the Earth Mother as a "flowing" principle of action and embodiment. When we are truly living in alignment with our dán, we are holding the energy of the Earth Mother, and carrying it forth into the world as a "flowing energy" as is illustrated in the image of the tribal mother, Danu.

* * *

The world calls us to bring our authentic and soulful selves into fruition. The process of initiation and the recovery of our soul-gifts that it implies is only the first step. After our spiritual death, and the recovery of our dán, we are called to bring this into the world, for *it is essential for the integrity of the world.*

In most, if not all, shamanic traditions, the shaman recovers his power by often becoming sick, or otherwise suffering a trauma that leads him into a journey through the spirit world. He suffers through many trials and ordeals, overcoming them, and eventually coming to face his deepest shadow. After he has passed all the trials, by choosing his soul over his ego, he emerges from the spirit world with a vision, back to his community where he will birth it into the world.

This is very much akin to the process of soul-initiation. There is an initial descent caused from a "soul trauma" which creates a powerful crisis, leading eventually to a disintegration of the ego in favor of the soul. This stage is followed by a threshold period, between descent and ascent, where the initiate gestates in the darkness, receiving a new vision of their life to hold. Finally there is the journey back up into the world, to embody and bring this vision to fruition.

Just as we cannot avoid the eventual confrontation with our soul, neither can we avoid bringing the gifts of that confrontation out into the world. This dedication to an engagement in the world, and the betterment of it, is the mark of an engaged spirituality. All too often people use spirituality to tune out of reality, rather than into it. To use the words of poet and philosopher, John O'Donohue, "Spirituality becomes suspect if it is merely an anaesthetic to still one's spiritual hunger"[4].

Our society is deathly hungry for an intimate contact with Spirit. However, before we can begin our journey to embody our soul and its gifts in the world, we must take the journey to own and embrace the contents of our shadow. The shadow is not "negative" or "evil"; rather it is simply that which is hidden from our view, from our normal waking consciousness. It is part of our unconscious that we have attempted to hide from ourselves, perhaps because we were afraid of it, or because we thought ourselves unworthy of it. Most people in our modern society have an unconscious relationship with their soul, and so their dán remains in the shadow.

We must be willing to enter into ourselves, and work for our own transformation, before we can ever work for the transformation of the world. In fact the very act of engaging with this process is a way of world-transformation. The self, as a dynamic interaction of the visible body and the invisible soul as a unified organism, is a microcosm of the wider universe. The world at large is a reflection of the inner landscape of our collective conscious and unconscious. In other words to work for our own growth and development, is to work towards the growth and development of the world. This is not a purely spiritual or psychological process of growth. It demands that we act in the world, and live our soul-destiny.

To step into your dán is to surrender your life to the shaping powers of the soul and of the earth. Your life no longer belongs solely to you, but participates in a wider community, turning towards service to humanity and the land.

To embody your dán is to live in service to the world. This does not, however, mean that it is a life without happiness or personal fulfillment. To live with dán and bradán aligned is incredibly fulfilling because it is living what you are passionate about, in a way that brings you alive. It is a deeper fulfillment of the longing of the soul. It is not easy however. Once you taste the waters of the soul, there is no turning back to the old way of living. To once more borrow the words of poet David Whyte:

> *No one told me*
> *it could not be put away.*
> *I was told once, only,*

in a whisper,
'The blade is so sharp-
It cuts things together
-not apart.'[5]

There is one more word that can be added to this weaving, which speaks volumes for the entire process we have thus far spoken of. The word is *dána*, and it means "daring" or "audacity". To face initiation, and allow the shaping powers of the Earth Mother to align dán and bradán takes *dánacht*. It takes a daring boldness to live the life you were born to live.

Endnotes

1. Whyte, David. *Fire in the Earth*. Many Rivers Press: Langley, 2002.

2. Monaghan, Patricia. *The Red-Haired Girl from the Bog: The Landscape of Celtic Myth and Spirit*. New World Library: Novato, 2003.

3. Whyte, David. *The House of Belonging*. Many Rivers Press: Langley, 2002.

4. O'Donohue, John. *Anam Cara: A Book of Celtic Wisdom*. Harper Perennial: New York, 1998.

5. Whyte, David. *Fire in the Earth*. Many Rivers Press: Langley, 2002.

CHAPTER EIGHT

Soul of the Body, Soul of the World: Initiation and the Reintegration of Nature and Soul

I would love to live
Like a river flows,
Carried by the surprise
Of its own unfolding.
- John O'Donohue, **Fluent, conamara blues**

We live in a time of global crisis. For the first time in our human history, we face the dilemma of the wholesale degradation and destruction of our planet. Such is the disconnection between humans and the natural environment that we have forgotten the fact that like the myriad of plants and animals who share this world, we are first and foremost creatures of the earth. In so doing, we have allowed our lives to become unbalanced and unsustainable towards the planet. In our forgetting of this ancient knowledge we have unwittingly repressed our relationship with nature, and thus a complete experience of soul to the unconscious. The enlivening presence by which we once lived our lives, has become dormant within us. It is as eco-philosopher David Abram has observed, "We are human only in contact and conviviality with what is not human. Only in reciprocity with what is Other do we begin to heal ourselves."[1] It is imperative that we awaken to the need for healing and balance in our relationship with nature.

The Celtic and druidic traditions offer us a great source of healing and renewal through an engagement with the natural world, as well as with the numinous reality of the Otherworld. The Irish terms for these, *coích anama* (which translates to "soul shrine") and *anam* (soul), suggests an interweaving of both realities as being our fundamental make-up. The very fact that the body was considered a shrine is a radical departure from many of the current religious notions; namely that the body, being earthy, is something that must be transcended in order to access the sacred. Contrary to this, it has been suggested that the Celts viewed the soul as existing around the body. This can be a profoundly liberating perspective. The body and soul are like a weaving or braiding of two threads into a single entity. We might say that our braid has become frayed at the edges, and has begun to unwind. A major aspect of what Thomas Berry refers to as the "Great Work" of our time, is the re-weaving of these two strands.

Initiation is the means by which this task can be achieved. Initiation is a process which involves a breaking down of the ego-self, which consists of our habitual patterns and limiting images of our self-identity; as well as a rebirth of the ego into a more balanced relationship with the deeper self, or the soul. This is a natural process which every person has or will experience at some point in their life. It is an imperative from the world of the soul, which asks us to dive deep within and seek there a more sustainable vision of our life. In many earthcentered societies this rite of passage would have been a natural stopping place on the path of life. We have lost our maps though, and so many of us wander, lost and confused on what C.G. Jung called the "night-sea voyage".

Using the triple spiral from the Newgrange passage tomb complex as a guiding symbol, a primal Irish map of this process can be seen, expressed and experienced in a variety of ways. MacEowen suggested a model, "Three Spirals of Initiation", the downward spiral, threshold spiral, and upward spiral.[2]

The downward spiral is basically a descent into the unconscious, and an experience of the breaking down of the basic ego structure, for the purpose of disposing of habitual and limiting patterns of behavior which feed the ego and deny the soul. This can be a frightening time, especially when, as in our society, we are not properly supported while going through such experiences. It is the death of an old way of being, which no longer serves the vitality of the soul. What must be understood though, is that this death will prepare the grounds for a rebirth of a more authentic self.

The threshold spiral is the period after the initial breakdown of the ego structure and a time of seeking a vision for a more "soul-centric" way of belonging to the world. It is at this stage on the initiatory journey when one encounters their *dán*. Dán is an Irish word with an interesting set of meanings. It can mean poetry, art, a gift or skill, and destiny or fate. Simply said, in this context, our dán is a unique soul-gift that each of us possess which we were born to birth out into the world as our destiny. This is the soul-sustaining vision that we travel the downward spiral in search of. If the downward spiral is our descent, the threshold spiral is our wandering in search of this new vision.

The upward spiral is the integration of the vision, our dán, into life, and the alignment of the ego into a deeper relationship with the soul. Another word relating to dán is *bradán*. Bradán refers to both the salmon, traditionally seen as a fish of wisdom in the Irish tradition, but has also been interpreted to mean "life principle"[3], that which nourishes and sustains us. Our life principle is the place from which we draw our fundamental nourishment and energy. Our bradán can be drawn from many sources, and not all of them are necessarily of the highest value to the soul. We can choose to draw our nourishment from life-affirming sources, such soul and nature, or we can draw it from our life-negating sources, such as our dysfunctional and disconnected society.

It is interesting, however, that this concept would be linked with the salmon. The salmon, in Celtic mythology, is a fish of wisdom, which imparts *imbas* (divine inspiration or poetic frenzy). The salmon is the symbol par excellence of the wisdom of the initiatory path. Their journey from the source pool to the ocean, and their final swim back up the river where their death feeds the life of the new spawns clearly reflects the process of initiation. Bradán suggests that the place we might draw our nourishment from is wisdom and our dán itself. It suggests that by aligning ourselves with our soul-gift – by living the story we were born to tell – that we enter into a deeper communion with the Earth Mother, the enlivening principle of the land, and the initiatory process.

Simultaneous with the initiatory journey are two other processes of connection, alignment, and reintegration, which work on similar levels. These processes are ones that assist us in aligning our lives to our soul as well as with aligning our soul to the soul of the world. They are parallel journeys, and all three work as a single process of healing and transformation.

A 16th century manuscript from Ireland, contains a poem which details the workings of what it refers to as the three "cauldrons of poesy" or the cauldrons of the soul. The cauldrons are like mediators between body and soul, ensuring both physical and spiritual health. They have often been compared to the chakras of the Hindu tradition, and perhaps rightly so, as they are very much akin to "energy centers". They are conduits for spiritual energy, directing its flow through the body and soul.

The first cauldron, the *Coire Goiriath*, or the Cauldron of Warming is our connection with life itself. It is positioned in the belly, and is said to be "born upright" in all people. The position of this cauldron is indicative of our most basic health. If the cauldron were on its side, we might be suffering from a threatening illness, or else be getting ready to depart our life. For the cauldron to be completely tipped onto its lips would indicate that we are in the process of dying. I would venture to say that what warms this cauldron is the energy of the Earth Mother, which can be regarded as similar to chi in Chinese philosophy. It is both a nourishing and initiatory energy. Therefore it would be accurate to say that the Cauldron of Warming holds and simmers our life force, and serves as our connection with the Earth Mother. The downward spiral might be thought of as our descent into the Cauldron of Warming. Interestingly enough the cauldron is often used as a symbol of initiation in the Celtic traditions, such as in the Welsh tale of the poet Taliesin. Taliesin gains his poetic wisdom when three drops from the cauldron of inspiration, which he was stirring over a fire, splash out and burn his hand. Trying to ease the burning, he brings his hand to his mouth and so imbibes the elixir he had been stirring.

The second cauldron is the *Coire Érmai*, or the Cauldron of Motion, and is our connection with the emotions. However, as alluded to in another translation of the term, "Cauldron of Vocation", it also contains our dán, or destiny. It said to sit at the place of our heart. The position and activity of this cauldron indicates the person's engagement (or disengagement) with their dán. The dán is activated by engaging with the deep longings of the soul. Just as we might think of dán as the Earth

43

Mother in motion, the Cauldron of Motion might be thought of as being the Cauldron of Warming in action; the essence of life's movement towards the fulfillment of the soul's deep longing.

Unlike the Cauldron of Warming, it is possible for the Cauldron of Motion to be inverted in the living. As Celtic scholar and shamanic wisdom-keeper, Caitlín Matthews points out, "In most people, only the [Cauldron of Warming] is operative, and the [Cauldron of Motion] is inverted over it, indicating a closed circuit of experience."[4] The text points out that the forces which turn this cauldron are joy and sorrow. If our dán is truly rooted in the longing of our souls, then it is revealing to note that it is the same force of longing, and the ecstasy of such an initiatory encounter, that is the driving force which can turn the Cauldron of Motion, opening us to that "circuit of experience". This is the energy and momentum of the threshold spiral at work, which brings us into contact with a renewed and life-sustaining soul-vision.

The third and final cauldron is the *Coire Sois*, the Cauldron of Wisdom. This cauldron is our connection to vision, poetic knowledge, and Otherworldly wisdom. It is said to be positioned in the head, or in the area of the third eye in many other mystical traditions. Like the Cauldron of Motion it is on its lips in most people. However it is through the turning of the Cauldron of Motion, that the Cauldron of Wisdom is able to turn itself. Here, like the upward spiral of initiation, we have the alignment of dán with bradán – our vision, the motion of the Earth Mother in our souls, becomes the new source from which we draw our essential life energy from. We shift from drawing on the ego, and instead drink deeply from the soul. With all three cauldrons upright and simmering, we become a clear conduit for the Earth Mother to express herself in our bodies and in the world.

To carry this map out one step further, we can also witness this same pattern of the three cauldrons in the cosmological map of the Three Realms in the Celtic traditions. The three realms of sea, land, and sky are often conceived of as the Great Triskele. The Great Triskele, as described by Séan Ó Tuahail in his *Foclóir Draíochta* (Dictionary of Irish Druidism) is a, "binding (which is indivisible and may never be broken down to three separate parts) [which] insures the integrity of the cosmos; as an individual binding it ensures slán [health]..."[5] These three realms, which as Ó Tuahail points out, are indivisible, and serve as a macrocosm to the three cauldrons of the soul-shrine. Like the three realms, the cauldrons are an indivisible binding which ensures the integrity of the body and soul.

Just as the Cauldron of Warming, is the life-sustaining energy center in the body, the sea can be seen as serving the same purpose to the three realms. It is the place of primal life-tending energy. In Celtic cosmology, as in the cosmologies of many other shamanic and animistic cultures, the three realms are seen as being bound together by a world tree, an *axis mundi*, which facilitates the hierophany of the sacred, of the Earth Mother, into ordinary reality. The sea is also symbolic of the unconscious, as are the roots of the world tree (in this case, drawing the water from the ground). Although we are always connected with the sea and the unconscious in some manner, we have a choice as to how conscious our connection and relationship to it is. We can choose to be asleep to this primal reality, or we can be awake to it, and participate fully in this realm of consciousness. The path to this waking up is the same path as turning the Cauldron of Warming; the downward spiral of initiation into the world of our unconscious, to recover the vision of our dán.

The land relates to the Cauldron of Motion in that it is the place of ordinary reality and ego consciousness; the place where everyday life plays out. It is literally the place of motion. When the Cauldron of Motion is inverted, and our dán is inactive, we have a "closed circuit of experience" to the mysteries of awakened living. This condition also closes off our experience of the land. When this cauldron is inverted we are closed to a true experience of ordinary reality because we have closed off the experience of the sacred and repressed it into our unconscious. Following our soul-longing deep into our unconscious is the path of seeking a vision of our dán, and opening ourselves to more expansive and conscious ways of life, rooted in the mysteries of soul.

The sky, like the Cauldron of Wisdom, is a place of vision, poetic inspiration, and wisdom. The sky can be seen as the realm of enlightenment. In the Celtic tradition it might be thought of as the place of divine inspiration and poetic frenzy. In this way it mirrors the Cauldron of Wisdom. Similarly to the cauldrons the process of awakening to life, of activating the Cauldron of Motion, leads eventually to the turning of the Cauldron of Wisdom, opening us up to the activation of our "poetic inspiration", and the dynamic balance between soul and ego, in which is held the potential for a deeper relationship with the Soul of Life.

The cauldrons of the soul are a microcosmic expression of the three realms, manifested in the soul-shrine of the body. The soul of our bodies is the soul of the world, and the soul of the world is the soul of our bodies; and this soul reaches out, encompassing all things within it. In this way we are fundamentally woven into the very fabric of life. As Tom Cowan writes in Yearning for the Wind, "The soul is not in the body, the body is in the soul. This is not easy to understand or to live. But we must try. If we don't, we circumscribe our life and greatly reduce the ways we know our souls, we strengthen the Great Split between us and creation."[6]

The "Great Split" is the belief that we are separate from creation, from the shaping powers of life. It is the belief that we are somehow outside the world, looking in. The truth is, however, that no such split has ever existed. It is the great illusion of our times, which tells us that we are separate, thus lulling us into a sleep where we forget our most ancient connection and relationship – that to the primal Earth-Spirit. The three cauldrons and the three realms teach us about the interweaving of nature and soul, the visible and the invisible. Through the process of aligning with these realities we are aligning with soul and nature, and awakening to the Soul of Life.

Initiation is the movement which brings these realities into alignment within ourselves. This process is nothing more than the journey towards wholeness; towards the fulfilling of our potential as fully realized human beings. It is the process of waking up to our dán and living in alignment with it. This is the doorway, or threshold, to an authentic relationship with both nature and soul as a single weave.

When we wake up to the presence of nature, we are also waking up to the presence of soul. They are intricately woven together, and relationship with one requires us to relate in some way to the other. Any attempt to know and work with the soul, which does not know and work with nature as well is fundamentally incomplete. Just as one cannot not understand what it means to be human without taking into account the wider relationship it has to the landscape from which it was birthed, we cannot understand the human soul without understanding the more expansive soul of nature, in which it dwells.

There is a story in the Irish tradition of Cormac mac Art, and his journey to the Otherworldly Land of Truth where he sees the well of wisdom. The image of this well is a potent one, and points to certain fundamental orientations of the Celtic soul. Swimming within it are five salmon, which eat the hazelnuts that fall from the nine trees around it. Flowing forth from the well are five streams. Manannan, the god of the sea, and thus an Otherworldly figure, tells Cormac that the five streams are the physical senses. He says that all people drink from the streams, but that only poets and the aois dana drink from both the streams and the well. Just as one can see the five streams of the senses as having their source in the well, one can also take another perspective, and instead use the streams as pathways back to the well itself. In other words, the simple process of being physically present and awake to nature through our senses, is a viable doorway to accessing the dimensions of the soul.

To be truly present with nature however, we are required to slow down, and develop mindfulness to the world around us. Our modern world has compelled us to shut down our senses in some very traumatic ways. Our fast-paced lives do not afford us the luxury of a deep and sensual relationship to the physical world. By staying locked into our own limited and self-confined patterns of tuning out of the world we close ourselves off to any sense of authentic relationship to the soul of life; in effect we replay the patterns of soul-repression that have contributed to the "Great Split", or "Wounded Soul" as I have come to call it.

What the world needs in this time of unprecedented crisis, both on personal and global levels, is a waking up to the sacredness of life; in effect, a global initiation and re-alignment between soul and nature. This is the world that we have inherited, and it is up to us to decide in what condition the future generations of the earth will inherit it in their own turn. We each hold the potential for waking up and blending with the soul of life. All it takes is a single draught from the streams of the enlivened senses to begin our journey to the well of wisdom – the place where the *aois dana*, those initiated into the activated soul-gift of their dán, drink from. We become the aois dana, because we become ambassadors of the Earth Mother into the world.

We become in ourselves an axis mundi, a world tree, by opening our souls to the life-tending currents of the Earth Mother, and becoming a hierophany of this enlivening presence into the world.

Endnotes

1. Abram, David. The Spell of the Sensuous: Language and Perception in a More Than Human World. New York, New York: Vintage Books, 1996, p. 22.

2. MacEowen, Frank. The Spiral of Memory and Belonging: A Celtic Path of Soul and Kinship. Novato, California: New World Library, 2004. Note that this author's work is viewed by some people as 'discredited' on the alleged grounds of cultural appropriation, cultural abstraction, historical inaccuracy and presenting his own thoughts as ancient Celtic thought. In reply, MacEowen has stated that he has ceased teaching and that 'Frank MacEowen' is dead. However, if his work is read from the perspective of a personal journey of discovery our students may find some of his writing of use.

3. Ó Tuahail, Séan. Foclóir Draíochta. 1993. January 21st, 2006. http://www.adf.org/rituals/explanations/focloir-draiochta.html

4. Matthews, Caitlín and John. The Encyclopædia of Celtic Wisdom: A Celtic Shaman's Sourcebook. Rockport, Massachusetts: Element, 1994, p. 231.

5. Ó Tuahail.

6. Cowan, Tom. Yearning for the Wind: Celtic Reflections on Nature and the Soul. Novato, California: New World Library, 2003, p. 6.

Further Reading
FOR WEAVING THE SOUL AND SOUL OF THE BODY, SOUL OF THE WORLD

Berry, Thomas. *The Great Work: Our Way into the Future.* New York, New York: Random House, 1999.

Metzner, Ralph. *The Unfolding Self: Varieties of Transformative Experiences.* Novato, California: Origin Press, 1998.

Plotkin, Bill. *Soulcraft: Crossing into the Mysteries of Nature and Psyche.* Novato, California: New World Library, 2003.

CHAPTER NINE

Awareness Practice III: The Sacred Senses

This awareness practice is concerned with cultivating our senses to perceive the sacred inherent in each moment. Often when the way we approach the day-to-day minutia of our lives is one of mindlessness –we close ourselves off, going from task to task until we have the space to relax. Usually when we are granted this space we choose to relax in ways which continue to contribute to a lifestyle of shutting down and tuning out. We watch TV or we spend excessive amounts of time at the computer. Neither of these things are inherently bad of course, but they do not foster the openness of spirit that is available to us in each moment of our lives.

Imagine another way of approaching your life and the world, one in which each moment is infused with a quality of the sacred. I do not believe that sacredness is something that an object, place, or person can possess. Rather, I think that it is a mode of perception, something which is going on at all times and which we can choose to participate in or not.

The practice is a simple one: start with just a single day. Commit yourself to openness; to relating to *every* thing that you do or experience throughout the day as infused with the sacred. Everything as mundane is tying your shoes and brushing your teeth, to the more profound acts of meditation and love-making. What happens to each task when it is infused with these qualities? What happens to your day when it is infused with these qualities? Now imagine that you lived your entire life with this awareness? What would happen to your life if it were infused with these sorts of qualities? Now live your life from there. That of course is easier said than done. But it is a practice, like any other. This is part of what we have talked about as "warrior training" fearless cultivation of openness, gentleness, and mindfulness. Just like the practice of meditation, when you try to live your life from here, your mind will sometimes wander away. When you notice this happened, simply return your awareness to the sacred, like your return the mind to the breath during meditation practice.

CHAPTER TEN

The Song of the Earth:
The healing Power of Music

To him that farthest went away, the sweetest music
he ever heard was 'Come Home'.[1]
- Old Gaelic Proverb

Music is a doorway into the realm of the soul. Hidden in the secret discourse of its tonality is all that has shaped a piece of music. Through the act of listening we participate directly in the soul of the song, vicariously experiencing the depths from which it has arose through the player. This experience is not indirect, nor does it take place in the imagination only. One has only to listen to a truly powerful composition to understand the suggestive resonance that music has. It was not long after our early human ancestors developed the capacity for language that music began to develop as well. There is something about music that connects us more deeply to each other and the world than language could ever articulate.

The presence of the spiritual in music is something recognized by all ancient cultures. Celtic mythological sources are full of references to music in relation to the spiritual and the Otherworld. Music serves as an archetype in the sense that it is a recurring mythopoetic theme or "image" pointing to a collective experience of the human soul. In Celtic mythology this theme is music as a doorway or threshold to the Otherworld, and the transformation towards wholeness that comes with such an encounter.

A prime example of this theme is the story of *Imram Brain maic Febail*, or the Voyage of Bran mac Febal. The story begins with Bran about his stronghold, hearing the sound of music behind him. Whenever Bran would look back he would see no one, but still the music would be there. Finally, such was the sweetness of the music that it lulled him to sleep. When Bran awoke there was a silver branch with white blossoms laying near him. He took the branch back to his royal house, where there is a mysterious woman waiting. She goes on to describe the music filled Otherworld over the sea, imploring Bran to travel to the Land of Women. She takes the silver branch with her when she leaves, and the next day Bran sets out with a company in a small boat to travel through the Otherworld in search of the Land of Women.

It is necessary here to say a few words about the Otherworld. Its description in mythology can be deceiving. It is often described as being across the waves, at the bottom of a lake, deep in caves, or under hills. To take this literally however would be a gross misconception. Although these descriptions accurately portray its imminence (the Otherworld is *part* of this world, not a wholly incorporeal transcendent reality), a literal reading would suggest that the Otherworld is very distant.

John O'Donohue, an Irish poet-philosopher from Conamara is keen to remind us that "the body is in the soul"[2]. The Otherworld is like the soul of nature. It is not trapped within it, but rather penetrates its depths, and wraps itself around the world. As we move through the world, we move through this nature-soul, and a dynamic openness of spirit, a soft gaze, and a gentle step allows us to move with the rhythm of its fluency. The Otherworld is the interiority of place, just as the human soul is the interiority of an individual. This is not to say it is "inside", but rather that it is hidden and invisible, and its depths cannot be penetrated by ordinary means.

The Otherworld embraces and reconciles duality. In another *Imramma*, The Voyage of Maelduin, one of the islands visited displays this well. On this island there are two flocks of sheep, one white and one black. Every so often the shepherd takes one of the white sheep, and places it in the black flock. The sheep turns black. He does the same thing with a black sheep, and it turns white. On this island, the duality of black and white is reconciled, and it is demonstrated how things are far more shifting and fluid than that. This then is the nature of the Otherworld; it reconciles duality[3].

Due to this nature of the Otherworld it would be impossible to say that it is very distant, because in the same breath we must also acknowledge the closeness of the Otherworld. To dwell solely in either of the two extremes would be to deny its own nature. Certain psychologies might tend to identify the Otherworld with our psyche; the inner realm of the human mind and soul, and that the going-ons there are reflective of our own processes. Other people might lean towards the more spiritual or mystical understanding of the Otherworld as an actual place, a spirit-world, inhabited by very real beings. However, I think that neither of these views are incorrect. Both are attempts to pigeonhole the Otherworld into one or another extreme; real or imaginary. We have seen from the island of the black and white sheep, however, that the distance between these seeming opposites is only as far as the other flock. What is actually important is that no matter how we understand the Otherworld, in all the stories in which it plays a part, those who experience it are transformed.

Music is forever leading people into the Otherworld in Celtic stories. Just like in the Voyage of Bran, we can see this theme play out from the ancient myths down to the folklore of the modern day. Music often plays the part of signifying that the faery people, inhabitants of the Otherworld, are close; the Faery music comes when the two worlds touch. Even as late as the early 20th century, as noted by folklorist W.Y. Evans-Wentz, there were musicians who were said to have gone to the faery people to become musicians. One such musician who's reputation is entwined with the faery people and the Otherworld is the famous harper, Turlough O'Carolan. O'Carolan was struck blind by smallpox when he was eighteen years old, and was soon taken in by the Mac Dermot Roe family, where he learned his harping skills. However, before Turlough ever even lost his sight, he was said to spend time at a local, *rath* or faery fort. After Turlough lost his sight he would ask friends or family members to lead him up there, where he would lay stretched out in a trance-like state. He later communicated a vision of having gone to the faery folk and learned one of his famous songs.[4]

An even more recent example comes from the Blasket Islands, off the west coast of the Dingle Peninsula, or *Corca Dhuibhne* as it is called in Irish. The Blasket Islands were a small island community, inhabited up until the 1950's when they were officially evacuated. There is a song from the Blaskets called *Port na bPúcaí*, the Tune of the Fairies. According to the folklore of the islands, this song was first heard by the people living on *Inis Mhic Uibhleáin*. Although it has been suggested that the origins of the tune is the sound which the singing of humpback whales makes when it reverberates through the canvas used in the island-dwellers boats. This of course doesn't take into account the fact that words were heard with the song, "*Is bean ón slua sí mé a tháinig thar toinn...*" ("I am a fairy woman who has come across the sea...").[5] Perhaps it was the faeries, perhaps it was the song of whales – or perhaps it was both.

Celtic mythology reveals music to be a great healing power, an aspect of the transformative nature of contact with the Otherworld. Caitlín Matthews, a well-known scholar and practitioner of the shamanic undercurrents of the Celtic spiritual traditions, refers to this process as soul-restoration. She writes, "Music plays the central role in Celtic soulrestoration, forming the most subtle net to help the soul parts reassemble. There are numerous examples of the silver branch's ability to bring the sleep of vision or forgetfulness."[6]

Dagda's harp, and the three strains of music is a prime example of this. There are variations of this story, as is typical of oral traditions. One version of the story recount that the Dagda has a harpist who's name is Uaithne, the husband of Boann. In this version of the story, Boann gives birth to three children which are named *Goltraí* (sad song), *Gentraí* (happy song), and *Suantraí* (lullaby). Each grow up to be famous harpers who excel in the respective music of their name.

These three strains of music were learned and played by all harpers, and used to confer those states onto the listeners. The strain of joy was not just a song of happiness; it was capable of conferring that happiness onto the listener. Likewise for the strains of sorrow and sleep. This demonstrates an interesting approach and philosophy of healing. In Western psychological traditions, healing is often though to occur by means of bringing a person from sorrow to joy. However, as we have seen, the Celtic approach brings a third factor into play: sleep.

Sleep plays an important role in the process of healing. A major example of this comes from the Ulster cycle of tales surrounding the hero Cuchulainn. When Cuchulainn goes from Samhain (November 1st) to Imbolc (February 1st) without sleep, defending Ulster from attacks, he is approached by his divine father, Lugh.

Lugh sends him to sleep for three days, while he fights on in Cuchulainn's stead. When he awakens he is fully recovered, and ready for battle again.

Tom Cowan, speaks of this power of sleep in his book *Yearning for the Wind: Celtic Reflections on Nature and the Soul*: "Perhaps the music of sleep is required to produce the tranquil state *beyond* joy and sorrow, a preview of the ultimate consciousness in which all dualities are reconciled, a brief glimpse of the dreamland where the tension between opposites is transcended."[7] Here we are again encountered with the idea of the reconciliation of opposites and its role in healing.

This fits in with Caitlín Matthews description of the process of "soul-restoration" as being the re-integration of exiled elements of the soul. This description fits in with a variety of other approaches to healing. One of these is the shamanic practice of soul retrieval. Soul retrieval is a reaction to soul loss, which is caused by a traumatic occurrence, which forces a portion of the soul to leave the person, in order to protect itself and preserve the integrity of the overall soul. We can see a more materialistic view of this in modern Western psychology's understanding of dissociation and post-traumatic stress disorder. In either case, a fragment of the psyche (the original meaning of which is "soul") breaks off to preserve the integrity of the whole.

Might this idea of the sleep-induced reconciliation of opposites also hold true for the bringing together of lost fragments of the soul? We are, of course, not just talking here of normal sleep, but of the "sleep" associated with trance states, and other altered states of consciousness that put us in touch with our own depths. The same kind of sleep that Turlough O'Carolan no doubt found himself in when laying in the faery fort, learning his songs from the *Sí*. This adds another aspect to the archetype of music as we find it in Celtic mythology: the striving towards wholeness. The search for wholeness fundamentally underlies the purpose of healing.

A second version of the story of the Dagda's harp adds yet another dimension to this archetype of wholeness and healing. In this version of the story it is the Dagda's harp itself which is named Uaithne. It is significant to note that the word Uaithne (modern *uaine*) literally means "verdant" or "vivid green". The harp is responsible for keeping the seasons in order, and importantly when it is stolen by the Fomorians, spirits of the chaotic and destructive powers of nature, they are unable to play it. This idea of music as an ordering principle not only to our lives, but of the land as well, is central to the ancient wisdom which states that the human community is essentially a part of the land.

In Irish the word *tuatha* has a double meaning, which is reflective of this understanding. It means both the people or tribe and the land. This is different than the more common Irish word, *talamh* which also means land. The original connotation of tuatha perhaps is *land as place*, a more ensouled presence than talamh might suggest. In this sort of understanding the earth and the people are one. It makes sense then that music would be the force behind keeping both the human soul and the soul of the land in order.

Where does this power in music come from though? Perhaps it has its roots in the fact that music is so primal in its expression of the relationship between the humans and the land. Music is a marriage between these two, and we can see this in the melodies and tunes of traditional Irish music. John O'Donohue writes, "Ireland has a great store of traditional music and there is a great diversity of style and nuance. Each region has a distinctive tradition. One can hear the contours of the landscape shape the tonality and spirit of the music. The memory of the people is echoed in the music."[8] Here again we have the reconciliation of perceived opposites in music. The restorative power of music comes from this nature to transcend the split between humans and the land and to unite them in sound.

The relationship between humans and the earth is both the most primal of all relationships as well as the most neglected of modern ones. It is not without reason that earth-honoring cultures consider the land to be a goddess; we were literally born out of the earth. One of the most defining characteristics of our time is the repression of this relationship, something relatively recent in light of the length of human existence. Soul and nature, the inner and outer landscapes, are one; they are the wildness of the world and the wildness of the self. To alienate ourselves from one is to alienate ourselves from both. In cutting ourselves off from nature we have cut ourselves off from the inner landscape of our soul, and so have lost touch with any viable and life-affirming definition and experience of sanity. This explains much of our modern world and our own culture-wide self-destructive behavior.

Ralph Metzner, a leading theorist in the field of ecopsychology refers to this modern relationship between humans and nature as being dissociative. Once again we are confronted with the theme of dissociation that we came across in discussion of soul-restoration and the shamanic practice of soul retrievals in the individual context.

If music has the power to heal us individually, to reconcile those lost elements of the soul, then it is not such a stretch to consider that music might form the basis of a practice to heal the dissociation between humans and nature as well. After all, as we have seen, the Otherworldly nature of music transcends and includes both dimensions, and so serves as a threshold or liminal space between both; the place where healing can be mediated from.

We have seen that music acts as a gate or doorway into the Otherworld. It was music which lulled Bran mac Febal to sleep, only to awaken to find a silver branch which he would follow into the Otherworld. Bran took the step that we are all asked to take. He was asked to seek out the Otherworld, and to find the Land of Women.

The Land of Women, and the mysterious woman who set him on his quest, may serve here as an image of Bran's *anima*. Anima is the Latin word for soul, which was later used by C.G. Jung to describe the feminine archetype of otherness in the masculine consciousness (the *animus* being the masculine archetype of otherness in the feminine consciousness). The anima or animus often serves as a soul-guide into the depths of the psyche. Jung described the process of integrating this archetype into the psyche, which ultimately is a process striving towards wholeness and the refinement of the ego consciousness into synchronous rhythm with the deeper self or soul. It was the sound of the music of the Otherworld, which literally woke him up to this woman – his anima.

This sort of perspective on the place of the healing power of music, nature, soul, and the Otherworld in psychology would take a massive shift in perception. Our materialistic and industrial based models of reality would not be able to accommodate such thinking, let alone practices. To live life from this sort of truth would require us to acknowledge the needed reciprocity between this world and the Otherworld, inner and outer, humans and nature. However, this sort of recognition of the interconnectedness of all things is exactly what is needed to heal the perceptive split between these realities. To do this we need to cultivate the ears of sacred listening that can hear the profound music of the Otherworld and bring our fragmented soul back into the wholeness of the soul of life.

Endnotes

1. Ralls, Dr. Karen. "The Spiritual Dimension of Music: Music and the Celtic Otherworld". Ancient Quest. 2000. March 26th, 2006.
http://www.ancientquest.com/deeper/2000-krm-music.html

2. O'Donohue, John. *Divine Beauty: The Invisible Embrace*. London, England: Bantam Books, 2003. p. 216

3. Mattews, Caitlín. *The Celtic Book of the Dead: A Guide for Your Voyage to the Celtic Otherworld*. Rochester, England: Grange Books, 2001. p. 46

4. Cowan, Tom. *Fire in the Head: Shamanism and the Celtic Spirit*. New York: HarperCollins, 1993. pg. 77-78

5. Printed in the liner notes of *Beauty an Oileáin: Music and Song of the Blasket Islands.* Claddagh Records Limited, 1992.

6. Matthews, Caitlín and John. *The Encyclopædia of Celtic Wisdom: A Celtic Shaman's Sourcebook*. Rockport, Massachusetts: Element Books, 1994. p. 325

7. Cowan, Tom. *Yearning for the Wind: Celtic Reflections on Nature and the Soul*. Novato, California: New World Library, 2003. p. 65

8. O'Donohue, John. *Divine Beauty: The Invisible Embrace*. London, England: Bantam Books, 2003. p. 75

CHAPTER ELEVEN

The Shadow and the Soul

The attainment of wholeness requires one to stake one's whole being. Nothing less will do; there can be no easier conditions, no substitutes, no compromises.
- C.G. Jung

The following section is a reflection on concepts which appear in Jungian psychology. However, due to their archetypal nature they are relevant to all individuals and cultures, and particularly relevant in the druidic tradition. This foray into psychology may seem out of place, however this is only so if one ignores the original meaning of the word psychology: psyche-logos – the study of the soul. Ancient nature-based religion was both the first transpersonal and ecopsychology. Druidism falls into both these categories. This should by no means be taken as an exhaustive study on the matter of archetypes. It is rather a very brief survey. A whole course could be taught on this topic, and for a better breadth of understanding it is highly recommended that you look into the books suggested in the "further reading" section at the end of this text.

Before we begin this work it is necessary to define the concept of the archetype. Jung described it as, "The concept of the archetype...is derived from the repeated observation that, for instance, the myths and fairy tales of world literature contain definite motifs which crop up everywhere. We meet these same motifs in the fantasies, dreams, deliria, and delusion, of individuals living today. These typical images and associations are what I call archetypal ideas"[1]. This is a curious observation, and points to what Jung called the *collective unconscious*, which is where archetypes are rooted. Because the collective unconscious exists at the deepest strata of each of our individual unconscious, these primal images can and do manifest within our own psyches as well.

There are several archetypes that are relevant to our exploration here. Namely, these are the shadow, the anima or the animus, the syzygy, and the self. There are countless other archetypes, but these ones taken together form a basic understanding of a circuit of process towards wholeness. On the Irish spirit wheel North is the quadrant of the battle between soul and ego; not over the ascension of one in favor of the other, but a battle into alignment and partnership. Each have a role to play. This exploration is one way of articulating and approaching the "battle". However, due to the archetypal nature of it, any approach is bound to follow with similarities and this can thus be taken as a foundational guide.

The Shadow

Jung said of the shadow, "The shadow personifies everything that the subject refuses to acknowledge about himself and yet is always thrusting upon him directly or indirectly – for instance, inferior traits of character and other incompatible tendencies."[2] There is a common misconception that the shadow is all of our negative traits. This is not true. Although the shadow, as Jung points out, is predominantly made up of inferior character traits, the contents of the shadow are truly *all* unacknowledged contents of the psyche –positive and negative. Although the repression of negative traits is probably obvious, the reason for repressing positive traits may not be as immediately evident. An example of repressed positive traits might be a brilliant and talented individual with low self esteem. They repress those aspects of the psyche which is proud of themselves. Reasons for this could be many, such as feeling the burden of fulfilling their potential. As the saying goes, sometimes it is easier to see our darkness than it is to see our light.

We all have repressed contents of our psyches, and thus we all have a shadow. The shadow is rooted in the unconscious, the "inner realm" of the Underworld, where soul dwells. That does not mean that it remains entirely hidden from our view. In fact, we see it almost constantly. We see it in our projections onto others. When we *hate* someone, it is usually because we are projecting our own shadow onto them. That doesn't necessarily mean the trait we are seeing isn't there in the person we are projecting onto. In fact it may very well be there, but what is infuriating you is that it is like looking in a mirror and seeing a part of you that you have been trying to hide.

The first challenge of the shadow is to recognize it and acknowledge its contents. The second is to integrate those aspects of our inferior personality into our conscious attitudes and to take responsibility for them. Neither are easy, and both involve working deeply with the unconscious. The shadow tends toward (but not exclusively) coloring our relationships with people of the same gender as us.

The Anima and Animus

It is both important and relevant to note that the words anima and animus are both Latin words meaning soul. That said, simply put, the anima is the personification of the feminine within men, and the animus is the personification of the masculine within women. Like all archetypes they dwell within the unconscious. These images are often projected onto members of the opposite sex, appearing in dreams and fantasies as the ideal lovers. I believe that these archetypes are at work behind the popular New Age notion of the "soul mate", and that the anima and animus are the true soul mate; the image of which is projected onto an ordinary reality lover.

It should be noted that this concept and understanding of the masculine and feminine archetypes are specifically geared towards heterosexual people, and that the contrasexual dynamics within persons of other sexual orientations are likely to be different. That said, this is the basic framework, and it seems to me that it is based more on one's own self conception of their gender and which sexual essence is in their core that determines whether the anima and the animus is conscious or unconscious (most modern theorists recognize that we each possess both, but one will be dominant and the other unconscious). So it is very possible to have a homosexual man who is more aligned with his femininity and thus relates to this archetype as the animus, or even a heterosexual woman who perceives herself to be gendered as a male, and thus relates unconsciously with the anima – in both cases the sex of their birth does not determine whether they relate to the animus or the anima.

Jung says that the role of the anima and animus is to, "remain in (their) place between individual consciousness and the collective unconscious; exactly as the persona as a sort of stratum between the ego consciousness and the objects of the external world. The anima and animus should function as a bridge, or a door, leading to the images of the collective unconscious, as the persona should be a sort of bridge into the world."[3] One of the interesting ideas here is that the anima and animus exist basically as thresholds to deeper stratum of our unconscious – the collective unconscious. If we accept that the unconscious is the realm of the soul then we might consider the collective unconscious to be a manifestation of soul. This makes sense when we recall that both anima and animus are words designating the soul. The anima and animus are the archetypes not of the soul, but of the intermediary between the soul and ego. When we speak to the soul or the soul speaks to us, it is with their voice.

Like the shadow, the challenge here is both in recognizing the anima and animus at work, as well as withdrawing our projections of it from other people, and having a more direct experience. Unlike the shadow which tends to show up in our relationships of people of the same gender, the anima and animus show up in our relationships with people of the opposite gender.

The Syzygy and the Self

If this process of working with and incorporating the shadow and the anima or animus into consciousness is reflective of the battle between soul and ego, then the archetype of the syzygy, or the divine couple, is reflective of the alignment and *marriage* of soul and ego; or the inner realm of the psyche to the outer realm of the ego. As such it is evocative of another Jungian archetype: the Self, or as he often termed it, the *God-image*. Both are personifications and representations of wholeness and integration, and are thus the "goal" of such process work.

How to arrive there (if one ever really "arrives", for it seems that it is an ever-shifting flow of experience and process, peeling back successive layers towards the Self) is another matter entirely, and not one easily given guidelines to. Because each person's psyche is unique the path to integration of soul and ego is also unique and there can be no simple step-by-step spiritual framework to wholeness.

The simple answer to the question however is that the path lay through the descent to the unconscious. The epitome of this process is initiation, which has already been discussed in detail. Usually however, one does not consciously choose to be initiated. It is an unconscious imperative set forth by the soul and experienced by the ego as a means of bringing forth a conscious relationship between the two. This is, however, not an advocation of maintaining passivity towards the process or the development of a viable relationship to the unconscious and the soul. Just the opposite in fact, the development of such a relationship, and the practice of taking active charge of your own process work will infuse the initiatory journey with awareness. Rather than wandering blindly in the dark, working with the unconscious will provide a map and a lantern which will allow you to navigate the difficult terrain of the soul with grace and fluidity.

So how can one work with the unconscious? The next few chapters will explore practices, such as dream work and shamanism which will explore and reflect on this theme further.

Endnotes

1. Jung, C.G., *Memories, Dreams, Reflections*. Fontana Press: London, 1995. p. 412

2. Jung, p. 418

3. Jung, p. 412

Further Reading

FOR THE SHADOW AND THE SOUL

Jung, C.G. *Memories, Dreams, Reflections*. London, Great Britain: Fontana Press, 1995.

Singer, June. *Boundaries of the Soul: The Practice of Jung's Psychology*. New York, New York: Anchor Books, 1994.

Stein, Murray. *Jung's Map of the Soul: An Introduction*. Chicago, Illinois: Open Court, 1998.

CHAPTER TWELVE

Awareness Practice IV:
The Elders of Nature

Everything is a spirit. This is essentially the animistic understanding of things. There is a quote by Father Thomas Berry which I like, and is relevant here: "The world is not a collection of objects, but rather a communion of subjects." The wind has its spirits, the trees, the grass, the mountains. "Objects" also are spirits; from drums and rattles, walking sticks, and wind chimes to coffee mugs and wall hangings. In fact there's little reason to believe that even the computer I am writing this on is not a spirit.

Certain spirits however, most notably certain spirits in nature, hold a different sort of space than others. We have talked about the earth-spirits in the Bardic course, which is a way of articulating a cross-cultural phenomenon in the primal Irish tradition. In Japanese Shinto religion it might be expressed as *kami*, in Tibetan Buddhism they might be called *dakinis*. In Ireland, these spirits were collectively known as the Tuatha Dé Danann, the Sidhe (alternately *Síth* or *Sí* in modern Irish), and later in folk memory as the Faery People.

When we talk about earth-spirits though, it is not solely the Tuatha Dé Danann that we are speaking of. The Tuatha Dé are earth-spirits, but this term can also apply to certain ancestral spirits, or the spirits that inhabit certain places in the natural world, or certain objects. I am particularly fond of a waterfall in Glendalough, Co. Wicklow, Ireland, which I recognize as a dana (nature) spirit. The simple definition of an earth-spirit might be, anything that invokes the quality of the Earth Mother or a quality of the sacred.

However, I prefer to use Patricia Monaghan's definition of the kami, which she uses to illuminate the idea of the goddess in Ireland. She writes that, "It describes these moments and places and myth and beings in which divine presence makes itself felt. The blossoming of cherry trees, a sharp outcropping of rock, the sun bursting through clouds: these are kami because they remind us of the order - the divinity - into which we are born. In Ireland, similarly, the goddess is experienced as a hierophany, a breaking through, of divine power into our human consciousness, with specific natural settings and moments as the medium of communication."

The practice then is this: go out into nature, to a place that is special to you, or which you feel drawn to. Go there with the intention of identifying an earth-spirit in that area, an elder spirit that serves as an ambassador of the numinous into the place. To do this, simply tune in to the place while you wander through. Pay attention to your feelings, your senses (both physical and non-physical), and where your gaze is most drawn to. Which features of the land seem to be "holding the space"? What evokes a quality of divine beauty that sings to your soul?

When you have identified that spirit, you might consider making an offering (I often use tobacco in the States or whiskey). Next, just spend some time with it. You might open up a dialogue. Speaking with nature is different than speaking with other humans. Obviously stones and trees don't speak English (or any human language for that matter). They have a different language. Much like we read a book though, we can read nature too – the shadows falling across the face of a stone, the rustle of tree leaves, the gurgle of a stream, or the singing of birds. These are all languages in their own right, and if we practice openness, and listen deeply with our intuitive senses, then in time these languages can become as clear as when speaking with old friends.

In any case, just the simple act of spending time in the presence of these spirits is enough. Notice how it affects you, how in the space they hold they seem to provide a doorway to the liminal, where we encounter the numinosity of soul. These are the real elders of the tradition. These are the real druids.

Chapter Thirteen

Thresholds to the Psyche: Dreamwork

One powerful way of working with the unconscious is through dreams. There are many theories about what dreams are; ranging from the purely scientific to the overly fantastical. Dreams can be interpreted in a variety of ways, ranging from the purely objective to the deeply archetypal, but for the purposes of this section of the course, we will be focusing on dreams as symbol-laden stories from deep within the unconscious. These are stories which are not only trying to communicate important messages to the ego self, but are also transformative experiences rooted in the unconscious.

One important point to note about dreams, which was made by noted psychologists such as Robert Jordan and James Hillman, is that in every dream the ego character (the *I* in the dream) is wrong. Dreams do not play the flattery game with the ego – they are meant to assist us in our growth and transformation. Because of this each dream serves as an invitation *and initiation* to growth and transformation by symbolically suggesting the ways in which the ego is mislead, acting "too small", or wrong. Dreaming is the soul's way of taking a magnifying glass to our mediocrity so that we might grow beyond it.[1]

There are several methods of working with dreams, a few of which we will discuss below.

Remembering Dreams

Many people complain of being unable to recall their dreams after waking. There are several methods that can help you to remember dreams. The most often cited one is of course keeping a journal and a pen by your bedside, and writing them down right when you wake up. Waiting to write down dreams is a problem because they quickly dissipate from the conscious mind. You might also replay the dream(s) again through your head, like watching a movie. Narrate the dream to yourself (or another person) in first person, slowly, as if it were all happening at that moment. All these techniques help to ingrain dreams into your psyche; to make the unconscious conscious, which is the purpose of dreams. Before going to bed, you might draw a spiral going inward, with the intention that you will have a dream (perhaps on a specific topic). The spiral serves as a potent symbol of going inward towards the unconscious.

Dream Interpretation

There is no code for interpreting dreams. A dream dictionary will help you about as much as viewing another's medical records will tell you about your own health. It is true that some dreams contain archetypal symbolism from within the collective unconscious, but for the most part a dream dictionary is only a waste of time and will lead to confusion. Rather, each symbol in the dream should be interpreted by the dreamer by way of personal association. After this analyzation of the individual symbols a wider perspective can be gained of the dream as a whole.

For example, let us say that you have dreamt that you have lost your glasses in a train station and the conductor won't let you on the train without them. The first thing to do before analyzing the dream is to consider your situation in the waking world. For the sake of this example let us say that you have just lost your job and are feeling stuck in life. You might interpret glasses to be a symbol of clear vision, train stations to be waiting places, trains as long journey, and the conductor as the doorkeeper between waiting and taking the journey. As such you might interpret the overall dream to mean that you are at the cusp of a serious life change (long journey) but will continue to stay at the edge of the cusp (station) unless you can "find" your ability to see things more clearly (lost glasses). As a transformative power this dream is probably trying to push you towards taking that step over the edge, to a life change necessary for the growth of your ego.

The Dream Journey

Sometimes our dreams remain obscure to us even after our attempts to interpret them. In such instances it can be helpful to journey back into the dream. This can be done in several ways. You might use the technique with the spiral described above to attempt to incubate a recurrence of the same dream in deeper detail (without changing the essentials of the "plot"). You might use what Jung called "active imagination" to speak with some of the dream characters. This basically involves talking to yourself. You take on the role of "you" in the dream (i.e. your ego consciousness) and let your unconscious speak as the other characters. You might feel a little silly doing this at first, but it can be quite a powerful technique.

Another option is to more literally journey into the dream, using shamanic techniques to enter non-ordinary reality, and re-experience the dream. With this method you can approach the dream in a more conscious manner, speaking with people or taking conversations to deeper levels with some of the characters of the dream (for example, perhaps the conductor could tell you why you cannot board the train without your glasses, or perhaps one of the people in the train station knows where to find your glasses). For more on shamanic journeying, please see the next chapter.

Endnotes

1. Plotkin, Bill. *Soulcraft: Crossing into the Mysteries of Nature and Psyche.* Novato, California: New World Library, 2003. p. 140

CHAPTER FOURTEEN

Shamanism and the Otherworld Journey

There is much debate on the subject of "Celtic shamanism", and whether Celtic culture can be considered shamanic at all. The term "shaman" originally comes from the Tungus tribe of Siberia, though scholars such as Mircea Eliade, have identified countless cultures around the world with their own variation of shamanism and shamans.

As Eliade defines it, shamanism is an "archaic technique of ecstacy". This is where many Celtic scholars disagree with the idea of Celtic shamanism. The claim is that Celtic religion was far more votive than it was ecstatic in practice. An abundance of such practices like the making offerings of swords and cauldrons to bogs and rivers certainly mark it as a votive expression of spirituality. However it also ignores a plethora of ecstatic practices, such the incubation of poetry by sensory deprivation and trance, to accounts of *imbas*, or poetic madness, as in the case of Suibhne Geilt. More than this however, the notion that Celtic culture was not shamanic stems from a misunderstanding of what the purpose of shamanism in a culture is.

As valuable as the research of Eliade and his colleagues is, it makes the mistake of misidentifying the major role of a shaman as a healer or traveler between worlds. These are no doubt true, but they are only partial and secondary roles. The primary role of a shaman is as intermediary between the human and natural communities; between humans and the green world of plants, animals, insects, birds, mountains, and bodies of water. The ability to heal the community, tell the future, or make judgements comes from the upholding of reciprocity between the community they serve and the natural world of which they are a part. The ability to travel between the worlds exists *because* of the need for this relationship. This adds a new dimension to our understanding of "Celtic shamanism".

It is worth pointing out that in Celtic society it was the role of the Druid to mediate the reciprocity between the tribe and the land. This role also fell to the one in the position of the sacral king, who was ritually married to the goddess of the land. But it is the Druids who were truly responsible, as they oversaw the rituals, and no king could speak before their Druid had spoken.

There could be (and are) whole books written on Celtic spirituality and cosmology as understood from a shamanic perspective, as well as from the angle of comparative studies to other cultures. That is not my aim here, nor is to prove that the Celts had shamans. It is enough that in the present, there are people of Celtic descent, living on Celtic lands, who speak Celtic languages, who are reanimating this ancient practice within the spirits of their own cultures and landscapes. No other proof is needed. Ancient or new, Celtic shamanism exists.

Another dimension of shamanic cultures often ignored by anthropologists is that although the shaman may have been a central (and simultaneously fringe) character of these cultures, the people of the community were also oriented to the same shamanistic cosmology and set of practices. Just so in Celtic society, the Druids may have been responsible for meditating on behalf of the community, each individual was responsible for their own personal relationship with the land and the deities. These people have been termed "shamanists".

Just as no online course, however in-depth it is, can make someone a Druid, it can also not make someone a shaman. That is not the objective of this section of the course. Rather it is about exploring shamanic practice from the perspective of a "shamanist". We are truly working towards the creation of what Tibetan Buddhist teacher and lineage bearer Chogyam Trungpa called an "enlightened society" then we need both shamans and shamanists. Both play crucial roles.

Shamanism is not a religion. Rather, it can be seen as a practice, a philosophy, or a way of life, which can be practiced alongside any religion. Even certain Christian theologians are starting to talk about and practice a tradition called "Creation Spirituality", which takes much inspiration from shamanic world-views, and recognizes that the primal vision of Christianity was very shamanic and mystical in nature. Whether you think the ancient Druids served shamanistic roles in society, or if you are just looking to compliment your practice with shamanism, it no doubt integrates easily into the primal Celtic vision.

Part of this ease of integration (as well as another point of correlation between traditional shamanism and Celtic cosmology) is that the cosmological structure of the universe is similar; both world-views include a tripartite vision of the realms. These worlds are generally spoken of as the Underworld, Middleworld, and Upperworld. In the Celtic vision this is Sea, Land, and Sky respectively, which we have discussed in the Bardic course.

Shamanism is closely related to animism which sees the world as an enlivened and enspirited place. Each tree, stream, stone, and mountain has its spirit and everything possesses innate consciousness and intelligence. This relationship to life serves as the backbone of shamanism. Everywhere we go we are confronted with consciousness. With this comes the opportunity for *relationship* with all things. Where as in non-animistic visions of life, a rock is just dead matter, to a shamanist it is a being and a spirit, and thus deserves our respect. When we can relate to all the world as consciousness it is as the prolific teacher, Father Thomas Berry writes, "the world is a not a collection of objects, but a communion of subjects."

Shamanism may be a derivative of the animistic worldview, but it is more than that: it is a practice. Shamanism is essentially a practice of altering one's consciousness from "ordinary reality" to "non-ordinary reality". This is traditionally accomplished in a number of ways, ranging from breathing techniques, drumming, the imbibing of entheogenic substances, etc. What works best for one person won't necessarily work best the for the next, and it is important for each practitioner to find what is most effective for them. Even the traditional method of laying down and altering consciousness doesn't quite work for some.

Certain people also have a difficult time visualizing, which is usually the way "journeying" is approached. To these people though, there are other methods of achieving the same states of mind. Use your body, feel or hear your way through a journey. For me, what is often the most effective is drumming. However it is not the sound of the drum that ushers me into an altered state of consciousness; it is the physical act of playing the drum, of opening myself and letting the spirit of a rhythm move through me that characterizes my shift in consciousness. Find what puts you in contact with your unconscious, and use that as a method of journey.

We journey for many reasons. When most people journey for themselves it is usually for healing or the discovering of wisdom that will help us grow into a more authentic relationship with soul. The ultimate goal of this section of the course is to lead you on a shamanic journey. The cultivation of this skill will aid you in the exploration of your own psyche (a word which means "soul" but is often translated as "mind" in the West) throughout this course and in your life. Below is a brief guide to this practice, presented in a "traditional" style of approach. Adapt it to your individual needs. For more in-depth studies, please see the end of this section for recommendations for further reading.

A Shamanic Journey

Start by formulating a specific question or problem you want to explore. Perhaps you have been experiencing a recent bout of illnesses, one after the other, and are starting to believe that they stem from a spiritual imbalance. You might journey to find the cause of these illnesses so you can correct it. Or maybe a love one has just passed away, and you are seeking a method to work with your grief process. You might journey for this purpose. If you are unaware of any issues in your life at the present that might be benefited by a journey you might simply go with the intention to connect with a spirit helper in the form of an ancestor or an animal spirit. Whatever the purpose of your journey, narrow it down to a specific question that you can hold in your mind, and use as a point of intention.

To begin the journey itself, start by readying a place to lay down and be comfortable and undisturbed for a period of time of thirty minutes to an hour. You might want to put a blanket beneath you and pillow under your head. Don't make yourself too comfortable though, because the goal is not to fall asleep. You can also sit upright in a chair, or crossed legged on the floor, if that is more comfortable for you. From here there are several methods you might use to facilitate the necessary shift in consciousness:

1. **Music**. This can be anything from drumming, rattling, or chanting, to a CD of drumming, rattling, chanting or even certain soundscapes. The music of such people as Steve Roach and Byron Metcalf has been intentionally designed to be "entheogenic", and to alter consciousness (recommended: *The Serpent's Lair* by Steve Roach and Byron Metcalf available through steveroach.com). A downloadable audio track of drumming has also been made available through this course for your use.

2. **Breathing**. Various breathing techniques can be used to achieve the transition to non-ordinary reality. One potent method is what I call the "fire breath"; deep rapid breaths for a sustained period of time. You might try alternating between the fire breath and deep slow breaths, in sets of ten (you can play with the number to find what works best). As you practice the fire breathing feel yourself transitioning. This could feel like a number of things, depending on what you associate a shamanic journey with. Maybe it feels like turning inwards. Or it may feel like going out, and leaving your body. One note of warning however: it is unwise to practice any sort of intense breathwork such as this, if you have breathing or heart problems without first consulting with your doctor. If at any time during the practice you begin to feel faint, dizzy, or a headache develops then stop the exercise, breath normally, and place your hands palm down on the floor to ground your energy. It is normal however, especially with the fire breath, to feel the effects physically, often as a burning or tingling sensation in the head (hence the traditional "fire in the head"). Simply be mindful to your condition and honor your limits.

3. **Visualization**. This method can be, and works best perhaps, when combined with one of the other methods. It is common for people to shift into non-ordinary reality by way of visualizing a gate of some sort; a physical doorway, climbing up or down a world tree, entering into a well, going through mist, crossing a stream, etc. These visualizations can act as cues to the mind that it is time to alter the consciousness in a certain way, especially the continued use of a particular chosen image. You might try visualizing such an image while doing breathwork, drumming, or playing soundscapes.

4. **Entheogens**. This method is not being recommended, but I felt it important to say a few words about entheogens here. The word entheogen means "revealer of the divine within", and is a term used for organic hallucinogenic substances when used for ritual, spiritual, or shamanic purposes. It is anything but casual "drug" use. Rather entheogens, in the shamanic tradition, are seen as plant spirit-teachers, and are thus given respect and honor, rather than being abused as they so often are in modern Western culture. When drumming or doing certain breathwork, the practitioner remains in control of their own state of

consciousness. However, when using entheogens you surrender that control to the plant spirit, whether mushroom or vine. The effective use of these teachers in transformative ritual or shamanic journeying requires the guidance of a seasoned practitioner who is capable of guiding such work. Unfortunately due to their illegal status, in most cases, elders – who possess the wisdom of appropriate use for entheogens are hard to come by, and there are few legal settings for safe practice.

The actual shifting of consciousness can often take some time, depending on your state of mind when trying to journey, your adeptness at the practice, and the technique you are using. If you are unsuccessful in your first, or even several first, attempts do not be discouraged. Keep practicing. It can be a difficult skill to learn and is far from easy to master. Although the shift in consciousness can be subtle sometimes, it is likely that you will know when it happens. There is a particular feeling of "arrival". Your intention of travel is to the middleworld, so bring your attention there. At the end of this section is a brief review of the three realms to assist you.

Take stock of your surroundings when you arrive. If you "see" your environment with your visioning eye, what does it look like? If you are unable to see in this way, how does it *feel*? Seek out the base of the world tree here. At its foot you will be met by your guide on this journey. With the assistance of your guide journey to find an answer to the question that you formulated before taking the journey. If you did not formulate a question you might simply spend this time speaking with the guide who showed up for you. Remember that often the occurrences of a journey happen in a symbolic manner. In such cases, or when the events of a journey seem cryptic or confused, you might try treating them as you would elements of a dream.

When you are finished with the journey return to the place that you began. If you used a visual image of a "gateway" to arrive, you might cross it again as a cue that the journey is ended. However, this is not necessary. To end the journey you need only bring your awareness back to your own body. Slowly begin flexing your muscles, starting with your fingers and toes, moving to your arms and legs, and then your head. When you feel ready, open your eyes and sit up. Place your hands palm down on the floor to ground your energy. You will likely feel a bit odd and discombobulated for a brief period after the journey. Drink some water or eat some food to help with this, or engage in any grounding activity. You might want to take this time to journal about your experience, while it is fresh in your mind, if you are so inclined.

A Brief Guide to the Three Realms

Sea - As a psychological state this is the dark realm of the unconscious. This can be a place of both great fear and great healing. The repressed contents of our psyche dwells here, and so Jung's archetype of the Shadow (the shadow being something like a splinter personality made up of the repressed contents of our psyches; positive *and* negative) plays an important role. It is also the dwelling place of soul's roots, and thus contains our dán or soul image. As a spirit-realm, the Otherworld is home to the ancestors and gods and goddesses of the land, sea and sky. Its darkness is the darkness of the womb of the earth, and so it is also the numinous realm of the Earth Mother in her myriad of forms. *The imminent sacred.*

Land - The Land is perhaps the simplest of the three realms to understand, because it is the one in which we dwell. Psychologically the Land is our normal waking consciousness; or egoic consciousness. It is also a threshold between the Sea and Sky, and so a harmony of the influences from the other two worlds is important to a soulful life in the Land. The Land is the world of outward action and embodiment of the inner states of consciousness and the fruition of wisdom from the Otherworld.

Sky - Just as the Sea can be seen as the place of the imminent sacred, the Sky can be seen as the realm of the transcendent sacred. If we use Bill Plotkin's definitions of Spirit and Soul, then the Sea is Soul and the Sky is Spirit. It is the realm of poetic inspiration, wisdom, vision, and enlightenment.

Further Reading

FOR SHAMANISM AND THE OTHERWORLD JOURNEY

Cowan, Tom. *Shamanism As a Spiritual Practice for Daily Life*. Freedom, California: Crossing Press, 1996.

Cowan, Tom. *Fire in the Head: Shamanism and the Celtic Spirit*. New York, New York: HarperCollins, 1993.

Matthews, Caitlín and John. The Encyclopædia of Celtic Wisdom: A Celtic Shaman's Sourcebook. Shaftesbury, Great Britain: Element Books, 1994.

Stewart, R.J.. *Power Within the Land: The Roots of Celtic and Underworld Traditions: Awakening the Sleepers and Regenerating the Earth*. Lake Toxaway, North Carolina: Mercury Publishing, 1998.

CHAPTER FIFTEEN

Awareness Practice V:
Contemplative Nature Walk

Sometimes nature is a mirror for the soul. We see, reflected within the twisted knots of branches and the swirling patterns of the currents in a stream, a reflection of our own nature. I suppose it is not without purpose that we have terms such as "human nature". The simple act of just being out in nature can be therapeutic. Not only because it often has the tendency to relax us and soothe us, but because if we truly pay attention we might see ourselves more clearly in it, than we can see in our own reflection in the bathroom mirror.

Walking too can be a therapy. It has a way of "moving energy" when we are stuck, or limited by the confines of the walls of our own houses or apartments. The Danish philosopher Kierkegaard once stated, "Every day I walk myself into a state of well-being and walk away from every illness that would have me; I have walked myself into my best thoughts, and I know of no thought so burdensome that one cannot 'walk' away from it." There is a good reason that many psychologists, eco-psychologists and wilderness therapists have noted the wisdom of taking their practice out of the office and into the green world of nature. It combines the healing power of nature with the healing power of walking.

And that is where our practice here begins. Go into nature, the wilder the better, but if all you can get to is a city park, that too is alright. When you go, take a question, problem, or issue that you have been facing with you. Simply bring it with you, let your self be saturated with it, and just walk through the soul of nature. Notice what you notice. Maybe it will come within your own process of thinking and mulling the question over. Maybe it will come when your eyes catch sight of a mother duck tending to her children, suggesting to you that a solution to your problem might be to simply spend more time with family. There are no rules to how nature will mirror the contents of our own soul – it is a fluid and dynamic process that only requires our openness and willingness to come face to face with the honesty that it presents.

A Brief Note Before Proceeding

The remainder of the course deals with an Irish story called the Voyage of Maelduin. This story, like most *immrama* (Otherworldly sea-voyage tales) are thought to be a "Celtic Book of the Dead", similar to those in the Tibetan and Egyptian traditions. The tale in question deals with thirty three different islands, each one representing an aspect of the self, directed towards soul-encounter. Death, whether real or symbolic is an initiatory experience, and so this myth is a map to that difficult terrain.

This series of lessons are not an initiation however. An initiation cannot be performed on another. It is an inward imperative set by the soul. That said however, the remainder of this course is a deep exploration of your own conscious and unconscious self, and is thus process intensive. The goal is a journey to your depths, perhaps to have an encounter with soul.

For this reason, this section of the course may not be for everyone. You may reach this part of the course and not feel prepared to continue. Although the course so far has endeavored to teach many skills that you will find helpful in processing these experiences, you may find you need skills and guidance that you cannot get from this course. You may not want to "go it alone" but prefer to seek out the help and guidance of a seasoned practitioner who can devote the time and attention you might need.

Whether you choose to take the journey, choose to wait or not to take it all, or choose to seek outside assistance – ultimately is up to you. The college is merely presenting you with this material, and a series of exercises and reflections to help you on your way. It is up to you however to take care of yourself; to know your limits and to honor them, taking responsibility for your own psychic processes. The journey is not without risk, but the benefits of growth and healing you may reap are great. This introduction is not here to frighten or discourage you. It is here merely to speak the truth about the following, and final, section of the course.

That said, the recommendation for "taking the voyage" is to utilize the practice of shamanic journeying, active imagination (as is used by Jungian analysts), or a similar process of deep meditation that allows for work with non-ordinary reality and states of consciousness. Because something like that would take a whole different course to teach, and because the material of such a course is not necessarily suited to online education, we have touched little upon it here. Of what technique is possible to provide in an online format has been. If you feel you need additional instruction (recommended) then you will need to look towards outside resources. There are several book that teach technique as well as locally run workshops and courses facilitated by skilled practitioners.

Your mentor as well as appropriate college staff are here to provide what support we can offer. If you have any questions, concerns, or hesitations about this aspect of the course then please speak with your mentor. He or she will attempt to assist and advise you to the best of their ability.

CHAPTER SIXTEEN

The Book of the Dead

Many cultures have their own version of a "book of the dead", whether it is a physical text or not. The Celtic people were no different, and scholars of Irish lore have identified several pilgrimages and stories which are thought to have served such a purpose. The purpose of a book of the dead, in any culture, is to guide a person on their voyage from this world to the spirit world at death.

Death however is not just that final event of life when the body is cast off. Initiation is also one of the many faces of death; the death of the limited and self-confined ego self. During the initiatory process we spend time in the unconscious, which is simultaneously the Underworld. The difference between inner and outer landscapes is merely perspective, and it really makes little difference if one chooses to understand the Otherworld as a distinct spirit realm, or as psychological "place" or state of consciousness. Both, if traveled deep enough in the spirit of openness and fearlessness, lead to an encounter with soul. It is this initiatory process of "dying before dying" that can also be benefited from a "book of the dead".

The Celtic Christian tradition speaks of certain pilgrimage sites as being "books" of the dead. They were considered practice, in a way, for the later voyage of death. These pilgrimage sites were dangerous, both physically as well as spiritually challenging. One such site is called St. Patrick's Purgatory, a pilgrimage cave made famous by a medieval account of a knight named Owein.

Another such famous site is the monastery of Skellig Michael (*Sceilg Mhichíl*). Skellig Michael is a rocky outcropping off the southwest coast of Ireland. A pilgrimage existed there that led pilgrims through a series of dangerous stations. An interesting idea surrounding this site is that, in general, sites now associated with St. Michael were once associated with the god Lugh. One of Lugh's tasks is as psychopomp, a leader of souls to the land of the dead. Nearby of Skellig Michael is another smaller outcropping often called Little Skellig. It is thought to be Teach Donn, however, the House of Donn - House of the Dead. This certainly gives credence to the idea of a living "book of the dead" tradition of pilgrimage at this site, pre-dating the arrival of Christianity even. In any case, such pilgrimages are of an initiatory nature without a doubt.

This is evidence pointing in the direction of practices centered around the theme of dying. As we have seen, death does not necessarily mean the physical act of dying; initiation and the shedding of outgrown layers of the ego, is just as much a part of the death process as the shedding of the body. And it is in this spirit that we will approach our work with an Irish sea-voyage tale, The Voyage of Maelduin. The

Voyage of Maelduin is the second oldest *immrama* that survives, the first being the Voyage of Bran.

In this tale, which will be retold below, with commentary, Maelduin and his crew visit thirty three different islands. Each island represents an aspect of the self – some offer blessings while others hold challenges. Each island, which will be visited in non-ordinary reality as part of your practice, will offer you insight into process. Each journey should be taken with care. You will gain nothing from speeding through, trying to reach the end. Your resistance to any of the islands should be taken as a clue that there is something deep at work, and that you and that island, as Buddhism might put it, have karma together. The desire to quickly get through each island is a form of resistance. This doesn't necessarily mean that you will not be able to work through some islands more quickly, while others will take more time and process work. Just be aware of when you feel as if you really have worked enough with an island and are not simply trying to bypass it.

A final note before we begin this section. Most of the commentary as well as reflection questions that go along with each island is derived from the translation and commentary in Caitlín Matthews, *The Celtic Book of the Dead: A Guide for your Voyage to the Celtic Otherworld*. It was an invaluable resource while writing this, and most of my comments are mirrored or derived from what she had to say in the book. I have referenced her where applicable to quotes, but I want to make it clear that her work is the primary source for what you are about to study. Many thanks to her for such an inspired volume, and I highly recommend the book to anyone who wants to go more deeply into the details of this work.

The Voyage of Maelduin

*Note: It is worth noting that the commentary provided on this text approaches the Otherworld as **both** a manifestation of the psyche as well as a discreet and very real place. In the Otherworld the boundaries between inner and outer are blurred. You may choose to approach this portion of the course from either or both of these perspectives. Ultimately what really matters is how they affect you.*

The complete text of the Voyage of Maelduin manuscript can be found in appendix II at the end of this book.

Maelduin was born the son of Aillil Ochair Agha by an abbess of Kildare, whom he had raped in his youth. Shamed by this, the abbess sent Maelduin to live with a local Queen and King. One day he learned of his true parentage, and that his father had been murdered by raiders from Laighis.

He decided that he would seek vengeance for his murdered father, and went to consult the druid, Nuca. Nuca instructed him to build a curragh (type of small Irish boat, made from skins), and to set sail with seventeen companions. Amongst his chosen companions were his friends, German and Diurán. As they set sail however, Maelduin's three foster-brothers swam out to the boats, desiring to accompany the crew. Although Maelduin knew that their presence would be inauspicious, he did not wish for them to drown, and so he allowed them to join.

They sailed to an island fortress, where they heard on the wind, the voices of the raiders boasting of their deeds. They heard them speak of the murder of Aillil, and the crew rejoiced at the vengeance they would bring. As they neared the island however, a strong wind came and blew them from the island, off their course. The following is the tale of the Voyage of Maelduin, and the Otherworldly journey on which he and his crew unintentionally embark.

1. Island of Giant Ants - On the first island, the crew encounters a land of giant ants. They attack the boat, and the crew steers away. At the onset of the voyage, we are unsure. We approach tentatively and with fear at the path ahead. It is exactly because we are afraid that out fears are magnified and set upon us.
At the beginning of the journey a cultivated practice of fearlessness is important. What are the contents of your fears?

2. Island of Many Birds - At the island of many birds, Maelduin goes landward alone, bringing back many birds for food.
What nourishment is being offered to aid you on your journey in the form of blessings or gifts from the Otherworld?

3. Island of the Hound-Footed Horse - On this island Maelduin and crew encounter a "houndfooted horse", a dog the size of a horse, who attacks them. The hound-footed horse is another manifestation of fear, but this time influenced by the state of inner confusion that often comes about through such journeys.

How is confusion animating and obscuring your fear?

4. Island of Invisible Riders - On this island German draws lots to go on land and Diurán travels with him. There they encounter giant hoof prints, causing them to return to the ship. Once back they hear a horse race, and see the horses, but no riders. As Caitlín Matthews says, "The crew receive their first intimation that they are not the only intelligent species in this realm. At this point, none of them has the sensitivity to see the otherworldly beings who live here, though they hear voices."[1] The Otherworld is full of life, but initially we are unable to perceive it. We may never be able to encounter the fullness of the Otherworld, but it takes a slow acclimation before we can experience the myriad of intelligences that reside there.

What intelligences do you encounter on this island, and what do they offer (and ask of you)?

5. Island of Plenteous Salmon - After a week of starvation, the crew find themselves at an island with a house of a single sea-facing door stands. A valve on the door allowed salmon to be carried by the currents of the water into the house. Beds, food, and drink were laid out there for the crew. The salmon is a totemic symbol of wisdom and inspiration.

This island reflects the abundant nature of wisdom from the Otherworld. What wisdom is being offered to you at this stage of your journey?

6. Island of Trees - On this island, Maelduin pulls a branch from one of the trees as they pass by. The branch then grew three apples, which lasted and fed them for forty days. The apple is a symbol of the Otherworld. As Matthews says, "On this island the travelers learn to let their gifts and perceptions mature, an important aspect of shamanic journeying."[2]

How can you foster the development of your own gifts and perceptions?

7. Island of the Revolving Beast - On the next island they encountered a beast which was constantly moving and shifting its form. It threw a stone at the ship and pierced it. This island is representative of shapeshifting, a common feature of Celtic mythology. It also expressed a similar theme to many illuminated manuscripts in the Celtic world which show different animals shifting into others. This theme is *neart*, which is a principle of "divine shaping"; all forms are constantly being shaped and expressing continuity from one form to another. The piercing of the ship may be interpreted as symbolic of the wound from which a shaman is initiated.

What is your relationship with change? The purpose of the initiatory journey is radical change from ego-centric to soul-centric; how can you foster this change?

8. Island of Cannibal Horses - On this island the crew encounter giant horses which attack and eat each other. This is the third island with horse symbolism. The horse was an important animal in Celtic lore; it was a symbol of the land and of sovereignty and thus of the goddess.

How is your sovereignty embodied? Does your life move with the natural order of things, or against it?

9. Island of Fiery Pigs - Starving, the crew arrives at the next island. Here the island is hot, warmed by the fiery pigs that dwell there and sleep in caves beneath the ground. There are many apples trees, full of golden fruit, which the pigs eat during the day. At night they go back underground, and sea birds come to eat the fruit till dawn, after which the cycle starts anew. The crew filled the boat with apples and sailed away. At the last island the crew saw an image of the world in disorder, where things went against the natural order of things. On this island, everything is in its place, and the world is in balance. As a result of this, we see subterranean pigs (symbols of the Underworld) and birds (symbols of the Upper-world) in harmony. The fruits of this is of course the golden apples, symbols of Otherworldly wisdom.

How can you synchronize body and mind? In other words, how can you work to-wards ensuring that your actions are an expression and embodiment of your deep longing?

10. Island of the Cat - On this island, they found a fort, with treasure, beds, and a feast laid out. Atop pillars within the fort was a giant cat, which leapt from pillar to pillar. The men set upon the feast which was laid out for them. One of Mael-duin's foster-brothers asked if he might keep a gold necklace, but Maelduin said no. He took it anyway though, tucking it away. When he reached the middle of the fort the cat leapt down at him, reducing him to a pile of ashes. Maelduin returned the necklace, swept up the ashes and scattered them on the sea. The crew then left the island. Celtic law was very concerned with the rules of hospitality. No one was to be refused, often not even an enemy. The guest also had to obey certain laws of hospitality. On this island however, Maelduin's foster-brother steals from their host; a boundary has been crossed, and he pays for the mistake with his life. Even in the Otherworld there are rules and boundaries.

Contemplate your sense of honor and integrity. Are you actively living in align-ment with these principles?

11. Island of Black and White - The next island they came upon was divided in two by a fence. On one side of the fence was a black flock of sheep and on the other a white flock. A herdsman came, and every so often would take a black sheep and place it on the white side of the fence. The sheep would turn white. He would then take a sheep from the white flock and place it in the black flock, turning it black. Maelduin tested this with a stick. He peeled the stick so that it was white, and then threw it amongst the black sheep. The stick turned black. Everything contains its opposites, as is expressed on this island, which recalls images of the yin-yang symbol of China. All dualities are but an illusion; shift their position and they soon take on the color of the "other".

Jung's archetype of the Shadow as well as the anima/animus are both archetypes of opposites within; what are the qualities of your own otherness?

12. Island of Giant Cattle - On this island, the crew captures and eats a pig, while German and Diurnán explore more of the island. They come across a shallow river, and when German dips his spear into the water, it bursts forth into flames. Across the river they see giant cattle being tended to by a herdsman. When German tries to scare the cattle, the herdsman asks him why he is frightening the calves. German is astounded that these are just the young, and that larger cattle must be elsewhere on the island. The pair return to the rest of crew, and they sail away. Again we have the symbol of the herdsman on this island, a motif representing the guardian of the threshold. German and Diurnán were unable to cross the waters, across which dwelt wonders which they could not understand. Often there are certain boundaries, in our selves or in the world, which we cannot cross because we lack the skill or knowledge necessary. We are unprepared for what they will reveal to us.

Know your skills and boundaries . The way we grow is to lean just beyond our edge, to challenge ourselves with that (leaning too far however may mean "falling in the river"). Where is your edge and how can you lean just beyond it?

13. Island of the Mill - On this island the crew find a mill and an the old miller who worked it. The miller tells them that this is the mill of Innbir the Senant, and that half the grains of Ireland are ground there, brought by those who were begrudged.

What heavy aspects of your self, that no longer serve you, are you ready to "grind away", and be cleansed of?

14. Island of Sorrow - The next island they came upon was full of mourners, dressed in black. One of Maelduin's foster-brother was sent to the island, and as soon as he touched land, he too became a mourner. Two men were sent to rescue him, but they also began lamenting as soon as they reached land. Next, four men were sent to save the two, and Maelduin instructed them not to look at the ground, and to only breathe the air through their cloaks. They were successful, and brought the two men back (the foster-brother was left behind). When asked, they told the crew that they wept because it is what they saw others doing. Sorrow is a necessary state, but if we overstay our time there, we can become stuck in the pattern.

Releasing our sorrow is just as an important a step as the full embodiment of it. On the last island we contemplated what heavy energies we might be holding on to. On this island what can you do to release them?

15. Island of the Four Fences - The crew land on this island and find that it is divided by four fences. The gold fence contains kings; the silver one, queens; the brass one, warriors; and a crystal fence containing maidens. One of the maidens came and served them food and drink. After three days they awoke in their boat with no sign of the island to be found. Another name for this island might be the "island of vocation" or even the "island of *dán*". We might imagine that the food the maiden offered was their destiny or soul-calling. It was too strong for them at the time because they were not sufficiently prepared.

How can you prepare yourself for the encounter with soul which will reveal your soul-gift to you?

16. Island of the Crystal Keep - The next island they came to held a bridge and a crystal fortress. Each time the men tried to cross the bridge it would throw them backwards. A beautiful woman came out of the keep, to fill a pail of water from a well. She did this without offering the men any, and refused them any hospitality. As night fell, the music from a brass net of blades lulled the men to sleep. This went on for three days, before she brought them into the keep and gave them food and drink. She spoke each of the men's names. The crew asked her to sleep with Mael-duin, to which she responded, "You do not speak according to your heart, your words follow not your faith; but so that I may reveal the secret of the island to you, inquire of me."[3] The next morning they woke up in their boat, and the island was nowhere to be found. Could this woman of the crystal keep be Maelduin's anima? Perhaps when she spoke the men's names she spoke their true names. The men however are too forward with her, and move in too strongly.

The anima/animus does not respond to this, for it cloaks itself in the mystery of the unconscious. How can you relate to your anima/animus without violating its boundaries?

17. Island of Singing Birds - As the crew sailed on they heard a chorus of song. As they approached a mountainous island they saw that the song was coming from the birds who made the island their home. This is the halfway point of the journey, and as they enter into a deeper layer of the Otherworld they heard the harmony of the Oran Mór.

What is your own relationship to the Oran Mór? How can you let it sing through your life?

18. Island of the Ancestors - The next island they visited was small and wooded. A hermit lived on the island, who wore his hair as clothes. He was a pilgrim who found himself shipwrecked. The island grew from a piece of Irish turf that the hermit placed beneath his feet, each year another foot of land and a new tree was added to the island. The birds in the trees were the souls of his ancestors. Every creature on the island was given a half-loaf of bread and a piece of fish for their ration of food. The hermit foretold that all but one of Maelduin's current crew would reach home.

What is your relationship to both the earth and the ancestors?

19. Island of the Hermit - The next island they found was surrounded by a wall of gold within which lived a hermit. He lived off what was provided by a well: water, whey, milk, ale, and wine, depending on the day. There are appropriate nourishment for each day. Each was given a half loaf of bread and a portion of fish to eat. After three days they were asked to leave. The Celtic tradition has a long history of hermitage, and a healthy relationship with solitude. We often think of solitude as being lonely; the absence of social nourishment.

A healthy relationship with our aloneness however is what allows us to see deep within ourselves; a requirement of mysticism. How can you be nourished and find community in solitude?

20. The Island of the Forge - As the next island loomed upon the horizon they heard the hammering of smiths. They heard the voices of the smiths on the wind, speaking with ill-will towards them. Maelduin ordered that the crew row the boat backwards in order to retreat, but to appear to still be heading towards the island. When the smiths saw that they were further away, one of them ran out into the water, holding tongs with a red hot ingot of iron. He hurled the iron at them, which boiled the sea. In Celtic culture, the blacksmith was revered as an almost shaman-like figure. The blacksmith was one who using the power of fire and water could transform iron into a blade, or other useful tools. Essentially the blacksmith had the power to create a new spirit (in animistic cultures, all things possess a spirit, and in Celtic culture swords especially were honored for this, and thus given names).

As the blacksmith of your soul, how can you transform yourself?

21. Sea of Glass - Here the sea turned clear, and they could see the bottom and all the rocks below them.

How can your relationship with water grant you clarity of soul and intention in your journey?

22. Sea of Mist - The sea changed here, and became cloudy, as if made of mist. The crew worried that it would not hold the boat, and that they might fall through. Beneath the water they saw a countryside. A creature in a tree tried to eat the cattle that a warrior was guarding. The crew is being asked to trust in the Otherworld, even when things become confused and it appears that they can't. We are often as-ked to trust the soul even when it seems counterintuitive, and when we feel we are being led into darkness.

How can you cultivate the trust in your soul to guide you? How do you know the difference between the voice of your ego and the voice of your soul?

23. Island of Recognition - The next island they came to was high-cliffed, and when the inhabitants saw them approaching, they panicked, screaming, "it is they!". A prophecy had been told on the island regarding a slaughter by foreigners. A wo-man came forward and threw hazel nuts at them, which they gladly gathered up before returning to the boat. The hazel nut is of course a symbol of Otherworldly wisdom (recall the story of the Well of Segais in the introduction to the course). Caitlín Matthews suggests that the people on the island represent those who have completed only a partial *immram*, and thus fear those who intend to complete the voyage. The most fearful thing to societies rooted in the ego are awakened indivi-duals who trust in the intelligence of their soul. This island may be reflective of that attitude of fear. It is interesting then that this fear begets the hazel nuts of wisdom, which help sustain the voyagers on the last leg of their journey. Notice that it is no longer the fear of the voyagers that threatens them, but the fear of those who are trapped in their own smallness; something which the voyagers have overcome by this point. It is called the Island of Recognition.

Could it be that this is the place where we recognize the dichotomy that exists between the desire of the ego and the longing of the soul? Where do you stand in this dichotomy?

24. Island of the Rainbow Stream - Here the travelers see an island, with a stream issuing forth from a stone door. The stream arched up over the island like a rainbow, ending at another door. Within the stream jumped plenteous salmon, which the crew gathered up. Again the crew is gifted with symbols of wisdom to bring them sustenance on their journey.

What Otherworldly gifts are being offered to you to aid you in the completion of your immram?

25. Pillar of the Silver Net - Here they found a giant pillar rising up from the sea. A silver net hung from it, which allowed the boat to pass through. Diurán struck it with his spear, and Maelduin cried out not to destroy it. From atop the pillar they heard a voice, but could not understand the language. Often the gateway to Otherworld is represented by a veil, a net, or mist. The silver net represents the doorway they pass through to reach the deepest layer of the Otherworld.

As poet David Whyte says, "anything that does not bring you alive is too small for you." The world within the net is large enough to hold you. Surrender "anything that does not bring you alive".

26. Island of the Shuttered Door - The next island stood on an iron pillar. Atop the pillar on the island they saw a plough and a wealth of cattle, but could find no way to access the island, but supposed that it must lay beneath the sea, at the pillar's base. Wealth lay on this island, but the crew had no way of accessing it.

This might be seen as being representative of the wealth of the Otherworld and our unconscious which is hidden from us. Find the wealth of your deepest self. Unlock the door to your potential.

27. Island of Women - Next they came to a large island covered in grass, with a great fortress. Within the fortress was a house of beds, and seventeen maidens making a bath ready. A horsewoman rode towards them, declaring herself the queen of the island, and bade the crew to enter and feast with them. When the feasting was over, the queen told each man to take the maiden next to him, and to go to bed with them. Maelduin slept with the queen. The queen asked the crew to stay on the island, offering immortality. They stayed for three months before the crew began to desire to return home. And so they left, although Maelduin was reluctant. As they sailed away though, the queen fetched them back by throwing a stick rope to them, which Maelduin caught. After nine more months they once more tried to leave. This time however one of the other men grabbed the rope, and the crew severed his hand, thus escaping the island. This is one of many islands in which the crew encounter goddess-like anima figures. On the other islands however, the woman would evade them, and the island disappear. They were not prepared for this encounter. On this island however, they became trapped; possessed by the anima. This is always a danger of working with archetypes (whether you choose to experience them from within the psyche or as autonomous Otherworldly beings). The anima/animus is the threshold between the ego and the soul, the mediator between the two. Sexual union here represents an important developmental stage of working harmoniously with the anima/animus, while also warning of the dangers of overidentifying with it, becoming possessed, and projecting it outward (especially onto other people).

Remember the lessons of the other islands, and approach the anima/animus delicately, respecting its shroud of mystery. It will lead you deeper into yourself to the unconscious and deepest layers of the Otherworld.

28. Island of Berries - Next they came to a forested island where many fruit-laden trees grew. The task was Maelduin's to taste the fruit, and after squeezing some into a cup and drinking it, he fell into a deep, healing sleep for an entire turning of a day and night. When he awoke he told the crew to gather the berries. They watered the juice down to lessen the effect.

Take time to heal and restore yourself in the wisdom you have gained.

29. Island of the Eagle - The next island they came to contained a lake upon which was built a church. An old hermit lived here, and shared his sheep with the men for food. They stayed for a season. While exploring the island one day, the men saw an old eagle carrying a branch which was heavy with berries. They took some of the berries for themselves, and watched as younger eagles took care of the older bird, dropping some of the berries in the lake to turn it red. The old eagle bathed in the water for three days, after which it arose restored to youth and vitality. Diurán also bathed in the water, and like the eagle, became ever youthful. They took their leave from the hermit and sailed away. The very wise and spiritual are often portrayed as young and beautiful. One has only to recall the Tuatha Dé Danann, also called the Shining Ones, who were said to be an incredibly beautiful race. When the soul opens, the energy of the Earth Mother can flow through us. We become ambassadors of the sacred Otherworld.

In what ways can you actively mediate the life-affirming nature of the numinous, or the soul, into the world, making it available for others?

30. Island of Joy - Next the crew came to an island on which everyone was filled with laughter and joy. The third foster-brother was sent to explore the island, and he immediately joined in the inhabitants, forgetting himself in the ecstasy. He was left there, thus bringing the number of crew members down to the original intended number.

This island represents the ecstasy of the spiritual experience. It is of course a joy to experience, but we cannot stay there. Ecstasy is described as the means by which a shaman (or druid) accesses the power of soul and Otherworld. This state of consciousness is a means, but not the end. The deepest layer of the Otherworld calls us onward; our "ambassadorship" calls us forward. What does this ecstasy teach you?

31. Island of Circled Fire - The next island they came to was circled with a wall of white fire, which they could not penetrate. Within the walls where many feasting, beautiful people, enjoying themselves in music. These are the Sidhe, the Shining Ones, the music perhaps the Oran Mór. This is the deepest layer of the Otherworld were we encounter our soul. To be human though, as David Whyte writes, "is to carry the invisible as a hidden gift to others". To be human we cannot remain here, we must return in order to carry this gift to others.

To be fully human is to be an ambassador of what is contained within the white fire of the Shining Ones; our soulgift. Seek an encounter with your soul, and the gifts you possess to carry out to the world. Take a vision quest. Fast. Journey shamanically. Meditate on this. Do whatever you can to find the "image you were born with". No matter how incomplete the initial vision: live it, breathe it, and birth it out into the world. Now. Don't wait.

32. Island of Otters - The crew came next to a bird-shaped island, on which dwelt a man. They found him making prostrations. He told them his story. He was once a cook in a monastery, and had also been a thief, stealing from the church. When once he attempted to dig the grave of a sinful man over the grave of a holy man, the ghost of the holy man appeared. He was told that to continue would mean going to Hell, but if he stopped Heaven was promised. As proof, the grave filled itself in. The cook took his stolen treasures and went out to sea, but much like Maelduin's company was blown off course by a strong wind. The ghost of the holy man told him to throw his treasures over board, which he did. Afterwards, he found the island on which he now dwelt, where otters would bring him all the sustenance he needed. The otters did the same for Maelduin's crew, and as they made ready to depart, the cook foretold that Maelduin would find his father's killer, and that he would forgive him.

Let go of the things which no longer serve your vision.

33. Island of the Falcon - As they sailed on, the crew saw a falcon of Ireland flying overhead. The followed it to a small island, which looked much like the one they were intending to land on at the beginning of their journey before being blown off course. They listened at the door to the fortress on the island, and heard within the killers of Maelduin's father. They went inside, and made peace with one another. Afterwards, Maelduin told them his tale, and then set off with his crew to return to Ireland.

How has your journey transformed you?

Endnotes

1. Matthews, Caitlín. *The Celtic Book of the Dead: A Guide for Your Voyage to the Celtic Otherworld.* Grange Books: Rochester, 1992. p. 43

2. Matthews, p. 44

3. Matthews, p. 28

CHAPTER SEVENTEEN

Awareness Practice VI:
Becoming An Sìth

This last awareness practice is something that I have come to call "becoming *an sìth*". An Sìth, literally translates to "the peace" and it refers both to the Faery People, often called the People of Peace, as well as to the peace of the land. Becoming an sìth is a way of merging with the land, of attuning to the currents of the Earth Mother there. In the first article in this text, *Wild Mind, Wild Earth*, we talked extensively about the memory of places and the land. Becoming *an sìth* is also a way of tuning into the memory of a particular place. That said, it has tremendous value, both as a means of attuning to the rhythm of nature and soul, but also as a source of non-ordinary information that is stored in the inherent wisdom of the land.

In the Second Battle of Magh Tuireadh, when the invading Milesians (the Gaelic people) defeated the Tuatha Dé Danann in battle, the land was divided in two. Everything above the land went to the Milesians, and everything below the land went to the Dé Danann. This provides us with a potent metaphor for our practice of becoming an sìth: "the land beneath the land". In other words, the dwelling place of the Earth Mother, and of the memory of the place, is within the non-ordinary spirit-scape of the land, which we might think of as existing as a strata below the physical earth that we walk on.

To begin the practice, go to a place in nature that is special to you. Although it is quite possible to use this practice to connect with particular features of the land, such as certain beloved trees or stones, this time try using a more undefined larger area: a place. A particular patch of woods, a park, a rocky ridge in the mountains, etc.

Go there and sit down. Feel the physical presence of the place. Feel this for a while, and then shift your attention, as if you were moving through that layer of reality. Sit with this for a few moments.

Consider that the physical presence of the place, is the soul of the place, the power of the place. As if shifting to a slightly different strata of experience, begin to focus now on the soul of the place. Sit with this for a few moments.

Once again, consider that the soul of the place is the *numinosity* of the place, or the sacredness of the place. Focus your attention now on numinous quality that the place holds. Sit with this for a few moments.

Again, consider that this numinous quality of the land is the currents of the Earth Mother, flowing through and enlivening everything here. Shift your attention to the experience of the Earth Mother in the land. Sit with this for a few moments.

One more time, shift your awareness. This time however, recognize that by thinking of the place as *other* you are essentially separating yourself from it. Allow yourself to dissolve that barrier by knowing that you are in the same flow of the Earth Mother as the place, and that just as you are a part of nature and a part of the Earth Mother, you are merged now with the land. You are *an síth*. Stay with this for as long as you would like, continuing to notice what you notice.

The Voyage Home:
Afterword

The word "ovate" may come from the Indo-European root *uat*, which means "to be inspired". It is my hope that this course has inspired you; lit a fire in your head. I pray that it has inspired you to become the shaper of your life, and enabled you to travel to those deep places where soul and nature meet within you.

This course has been directed at fostering an enlivened relationship with the world and with your soul. If you are completing this course then you have journeyed deep and far. Like all pilgrimages, one of the most important phases is the return home, to carry with you the seeds of your transformation, and to plant them in your heart. The soul can be a harsh mistress; once we taste her we can seldom forget. We can seldom stay within the small and confining lives we once built for ourselves. When we encounter the soul it is often time to metaphorically "burn down the house", and to build a new one – a "house of belonging", to use David Whyte's words.

May you be blessed in the house of belonging you will one day build.

The breeze at dawn has secrets to tell you.
Don't go back to sleep.
You must ask for what you really want.
Don't go back to sleep.
People are going back and forth across the doorsill
where the two worlds touch.
The door is round and open.
Don't go back to sleep.
- Jelaluddin Rumi

Guide to Meditation

Meditation is a basic practice of mindfulness. Mindfulness does not mean a distracted mind full of thoughts, but rather a state of sensitivity and awareness to the presence of mind in oneself. Simply put, meditation is a technique of slowing down and cultivating the awareness to observe one's self. Because meditation is a practice, it is important to develop the discipline of actually doing it. Meditation is also a process. There is no easy step-by-step guide to perfecting the practice. It is something you cultivate. That said, below is an outline of a style of sitting meditation which the Tibetan Buddhist teacher, Chogyam Trungpa, called Shambhala meditation. It is a secular form of meditation meant to be part of 'sacred warriorship'.

- **The Posture:** Sit on the floor with your legs crossed comfortably. You may want to sit on a cushion to elevate yourself a bit, and provide comfort for longer meditation sessions. If you're unable to sit on the floor it is alright to use a chair. Keep your back straight and upright. Place your hands on your thighs. Keeping them on your thighs rather than your knees or resting in your lap will help straighten your back. Keep your eyes open, looking at the floor (or wall) about 6-8 feet in front of you. The mouth can be slightly open allowing for easy breathing.

- **The Practice:** is simple: follow your breath. Breathe in deeply but comfortably, then out. On each out breath apply a tiny point of awareness. Just for a moment become completely aware of your out breath. Because it is the nature of the mind, thoughts will no doubt arise. Without judgment of analyzation, label each thought that arises: 'thought', and then let it go, drifting through your mind like clouds. Visualizations are also thoughts, let them go too. Whatever you are feeling, you also do not need to "think" about it, or tell yourself the story of why you feel the way you do. Just allow yourself to feel whatever you are feeling without judgment or thought. You will know when your mind has wandered when you have either forgotten why you are sitting, or you have lost track of your breath. Label whatever you were thinking as: 'thought', and then return to your breath.

It sounds much simpler than it is of course, but stick with the practice and you will no doubt find it to be immensely illuminating. For a more detailed study of meditation and the path of sacred warriorship (a path which I think is incredibly relevant to the Druid path and awakened Celtic warriorship) I highly recommend: Shambhala: The Sacred Path of the Warrior by Chogyam Trungpa.

APPENDIX 1
Guide to the Pronunciation of Irish Words

There are many Irish words within the course, the pronunciation of which can be quite difficult. Like any language there are exceptions to grammatical rules in Irish, and so this guide should not be viewed as exhaustive. It is a brief guide to the basics of Irish grammar to help you pronounce some of the words in the course handbook. For a more complete study you might look into a distance learning course or one of the many book and tape study guides.

Vowels

Below is an approximation of the pronunciation of each vowel in Irish using examples of English phonetics. They are divided into long and short. Further, each vowel is marked as either broad *(b)* or slender *(s)*.

Long vowels
    á - pronounced like *aw. (b)*
    é - pronounced like *ay. (s)*
    í - pronounced like *ee. (s)*
    ó - pronounced like *ow. (b)*
    ú - pronounced like *oo. (b)*

Short vowels
    a - pronounced like *o* as in hot. *(b)*
    e - pronounced like *e* as in let. *(s)*
    i - pronounced like *i* as in sit. *(s)*
    o - pronounced like *o* as in done. *(b)*
    u - pronounced like *u* as in put. *(b)*

Consonants

Broad consonants are ones either followed by or preceded by broad vowels; slender consonants are similarly either followed by or preceded by slender vowels. Lenited consonants (consonants followed by an *h*) are also marked below.

Broad
    b - pronounced like *b* as in box.
    m - pronounced like *m* as in mail.
    p - pronounced like *p* as in put.

d - pronounced like *d* as in door.
n - pronounced like *n* as in naked.
t - pronounced like *t* as in tome.
l - pronounced like *l* as in lord.
s - pronounced like *s* as in stock (*fh* is not pronounced).
f/ph - pronounced like *f* as in foe.
bh/mh - pronounced like *v* as in value or like *w* as in wort.
c - pronounced like *c* as in coat.
g - pronounced like *g* as in guard.
ng - pronounced like *ng* as in hung.
ch - pronounced like *ch* as in a Scottish loch.
dh/gh - pronounced like a French *r*.
r - pronounced like *r* as in bar, but rolled slightly.
sh - pronounced like *h*.
th - pronounced like *h*.

Slender

b - pronounced like *b* as in beat.
m - pronounced like *m* as in me.
p - pronounced like *p* as in pen.
d - pronounced like *d* as in dean.
n - pronounced like *n* as in nit.
t - pronounced like *t* as in tin.
l - pronounced like *l* as in lip.
s - pronounced like *sh* as in she.
f/ph - pronounced like *f* as in feed.
bh/mh - pronounced like *v* as in vie.
c - pronounced like *k* as in kick.
g - pronounced like *g* as in gain.
ng - pronounced like *ng* as in sing
ch - pronounced like *ch* as in the German ich.
dh/gh - pronounced like *y* as in yellow.
r - pronounced like *r* as in rid.
sh - pronounced like *h*.
th - pronounced like *h*.

Source: Ó Cróinín, Breandán (editor). *Pocket Oxford Irish Dictionary.* New York: Oxford University Press, 1999.

APPENDIX II
The Voyage of Maelduin: Original Text

*Below is the full text of the English translation of "The Voyage of Maelduin" (Immram curaig Maíle Duin, LU, YBL, Harl. 5280, Eg. 1782). Translated by Whitley Stokes and published in Revue Celtique 9, 1888, 447-495; 10, 1889, 50-95. Missing text in the manuscript is indicated by ****.*

Illustrations from "The Voyage of Maelduin", published in "The Book of Wonder Voyages" (1919) by Joseph Jacobs.

The manuscript and the illustrations are in the public domain.

PROLOGUE

Three years and seven months was it wandering in the ocean..

There was a famous man of the Eoganacht of Ninuss (that is, the Eoganacht of the Arans): his name was Ailill of the 'Edge of Battle'. A mighty soldier was he, and a hero lord of his own tribe and kindred. And there was a young nun, the prioress of a church of nuns, with whom he met. Between them both there was a noble boy, Máel Dúin, son of Ailill.

This is the way according to which Máel Dúin's conception and his birth came to pass. Once upon a time the king of the Eoganacht went on a raid into another district and province and with him fared Ailill of the Edge of Battle. They unyoked and encamped on an upland therein. There was a church of nuns near to that upland. At midnight, then, when everyone had ceased moving in the camp, Ailill went to the church. It was the hour that the (aforesaid) nun went to strike the bell for nocturne. Ailill caught her hand, and threw her down, and lay with her.

Said the woman to him: 'Unblessed is our state'. Saith she: '(for) this is the time for my conceiving. Which is thy race and what is thy name?'

Said the hero: 'Ailill of the Edge of Battle is my name '(and I am) of the Eoganacht of Ninuss in Thomond.'

Then after ravaging and taking hostages, the king returned to his district, Ailill also being with him.

Soon after Ailill had reached his tribe, marauders of Leix slew him. They burnt (the church named) Dubcluain upon him.

At the end of nine months the woman brought forth a boy, and gave him a name, Máel Dúin was he. The boy was afterwards taken secretly to her friends, even to the king's queen; and by her Máel Dúin was reared; and she gave out that she was his mother.

Now the one foster-mother reared him and the king's three sons, in one cradle, and on one breast, and on one lap.

Beautiful, indeed, was his form; and it is doubtful if there has been in flesh anyone as beautiful as he. So he grew up till he was a young warrior and fit to use weapons. Great then, was his brightness and his gaiety and his playfulness. In his play he outwent all his comrades, both in throwing balls and running, and leaping, and putting stones, and racing horses. He had, in sooth, the victory in each of those games. One day, then, a certain soldier warrior grew envious against him, and he said in transport and anger: 'Thou', saith he, 'whose clan and kindred no one knows, whose mother and father no-one knows, vanquish us in every game, whether we contend with you on land or on water, or on the draughtboard!'

So then Máel Dúin was silent, for till then he had thought that he was a son of the king and of the queen his foster-mother. Then he said to his foster-mother: 'I will not dine and I will not drink until thou tell me', saith he, 'my mother and my father'. 'But', saith she, 'why art thou inquiring after that? Do not take to heart the words of the haughty warriors. I am thy mother.' Saith she: 'The love of the people of the earth for their sons is no greater than the love I bear to you'.

'That may be' he said: 'nevertheless, make known my parents to me'.

So his foster-mother went with him, and delivered him into his (own) mother's hand; and thereafter he entreated his mother to declare his father to him.'

'Silly', saith she, 'is what you art adoing, for if you shouldst know thy father 'you hast no good of him, and you shalt be the gladder, for he died long ago'.

'Tis the better for me to know it', saith he, 'however'.

Then his mother told him the truth. 'Ailill of the Edge of Battle was thy father', saith she, 'of the Eoganacht of Ninuss'.

Then Máel Dúin went to his fatherland and to his own heritage, having his (three) foster-brothers with him; and beloved warriors were they. And then his kindred welcomed him, and bade him be of good cheer.

At a certain time afterwards there was a number of warriors in the graveyard of the church of Dubcluain, putting stones. So Máel Dúin's foot was planted on the scorched ruin of the church, and over it he was flinging the stone. A certain poison-tongued man of the community of the church, Briccne was his name – said to Máel Dúin: 'It were better,' saith he,' to avenge the man who was burnt there than to cast stones over his bare burnt bones'.

Who (was) that ?' saith Máel Dúin.

Ailill', saith he, 'thine (own) father'.

Who killed him ?' asked Máel Dúin.

Briccne replied: 'Marauders of Leix,' saith he, 'and they destroyed him on this spot'.

Then Máel Dúin threw away the stone (which he was about to cast), and took his mantle round him, and his armour on him; and he was mournful thereat. And he asked the way to wend to Leix, and the guides told him that he could only go by sea.

So he went into the country of Corcomroe to seek a charm and a blessing of the wizard who dwelt there, to begin building a boat. (Nuca was the wizard's name and it is from him that Boirenn Nuca is named). He told Máel Dúin the day on which he should begin the boat, and the number of the crew that should go in her, to wit, seventeen men, or sixty according to others. And he (also) told him that no number greater or less than that should go; and he (lastly) told him the day he should set to sea.

Then Máel Dúin built a three-skinned boat; and they who were to go in it in his company were ready. Germán was there and Diurán the Rhymer. So then he went to sea on the day that the wizard had told him to set out. When they had gone a little from land after hoisting the sail, then came into the harbour after them his three foster-brothers, the three sons of his foster-father and foster-mother; and they shouted to them to come back again to them to the end that they might go with them.

'Get you home,' saith Máel Dúin; 'for even though we should return (to land), only the number we have here shall go with me

'We will go after thee into the sea and be drowned therein, unless thou come unto us'.

Then the three of them cast themselves into the sea, and they swam far from land. When Máel Dúin saw that, he turned towards them so that they might not be drowned, and he brought them into his boat.

That day till vespers they were a-rowing, and the night after it till midnight, when they found two small bare islands, with two forts in them; and then they heard out of the forts the noise and outcry of intoxication, and the soldiers, and the trophies. And this was what one man said to the other: 'Stand off from me', saith he, 'for I am a better hero than thou, for it, is I that slew Ailill of the Edge of Battle, and burnt Dubcluain on him and no evil hath hitherto been done to me therefor by his kindred; and thou hast never done the like of that!

'We have the victory in our hands', saith Germán, and saith Diurán the Rhymer: 'God hath brought us direct and God hath guided our barque. Let us go and wreck these two forts, since God hath revealed to us our enemies in them!'

As they were saying these words, a great wind came upon, them, so that they were driven (over the sea, all) that night until morning. And even after morning they saw nor earth nor land, and they knew not whither they were going. Then said Máel Dúin: 'Leave the boat still, without rowing and whithersoever it shall please God to bring it, bring'.

The Giant Ants.

Then they entered the great, endless ocean; and Máel Dúin afterwards said to his foster-brothers: 'Ye have caused this to us, casting yourselves upon us in the boat in spite of the word of the enchanter and wizard, who told us that on board the boat we should go only the number that we were before you came'.

They had no answer, save only to be silent for a little space.

II

Three days and three nights were they, and they found neither land nor ground. Then on the morning of the third day they heard a sound from the north-east. 'This is the voice of a wave against a shore', said Máel Dúin. Now when the day was bright they made towards land. As they were casting lots to see which of them should go on shore, there came a great swarm of ants each of them the size of a foal, down to the strand towards them, and into the sea. What the ants desired was to eat the crew and their boat: so the sailors fled for three days and three nights; and they saw nor land nor ground.

III

On the morning of the third day the heard the sound of a wave against the beach, and with the daylight they saw an island high and great; and terraces all round about it. Lower was each of them than the other, and there was a row of trees around it, and many great birds on these trees. And they were taking counsel as to who should go to explore the island and see whether the birds were gentle. 'I will go', saith Máel Dúin. So Máel Dúin went, and warily searched the, island, and found nothing evil therein. And they ate their fill of the birds and brought some of them on board their boat.

IV

Three days thereafter, and three nights were they at sea. But on the morning of the fourth day they perceived another great island. Sandy was its soil. When they came to the shore of the island they saw therein a beast like a horse. The legs of a hound he had, with rough, sharp nails; and great was his joy at seeing them. And he was prancing (?) before them, for he longed to devour them and their boat. 'He is not sorry to meet us,' saith Máel Dúin; 'let us go back from the island'. That was done; and when the beast perceived them fleeing, he went down to the strand and, began digging up the beach with his sharp nails, and pelting them (with the pebbles), and they did not expect to escape from him.

V

Thereafter they rowed afar, and a great, flat island they see before them. Then to Germán fell an ill lot to go and look at that island. 'Both of us will go,' saith Diurán the Rhymer, 'and thou wilt come with me some other time into an island which it falls to my lot to explore'. So the two of them entered the island. Great was its size and its breadth, and they saw therein a long, great green, with vast hoof-marks of horses upon it. As large as the sail of a ship was the mark of the hoof of each horse. They saw, moreover, the shells of huge nuts like *** and they saw, there, also great leavings (?) of the plunder of many men. So they dreaded that which they saw, and they called their people to them to see what they beheld. They were afraid then, after seeing what they beheld, and they all, swiftly, hastily, went on board their boat.

When they had gone a little from land, they beheld (rushing) along the sea to the island a great multitude, which, after reaching the green of the island, held a horse-race. And swifter than the wind was each horse, and great was the shouting (of the multitude) and their outcry and noise. And then the strokes of their horse-rods at the meeting were heard by Máel Dúin, and he heard, moreover, what each of them was saying: 'Bring the grey steed'; 'Drive the dun horse there'; 'Bring the white horse!'; 'My steed is faster!'; 'My horse leaps better'.

When the wanderers heard those words, they went away with all their might for they felt sure it was a meeting of demons they beheld.

VI

A full week were they voyaging, in hunger and in thirst, when they discovered a great, high island with a great house therein on the seashore and a doorway out of the house into the plain of the island and another door (opening) into the sea, and against that door there was a valve of stone. That valve was pierced by an aperture, through which the sea-waves were flinging the salmon into the midst of that house. Máel Dúin and his men entered that house, and therein they found no one. After this they beheld a testered bed for the chief of the house alone, and a bed for every three of his household, and food for three before every bed, and a vessel of glass with good liquor before every bed and a cup of glass on every vessel. So they dined off that food and liquor and they give thanks to Almighty God, who had helped them from their hunger.

VII

When they went from the island they were a long while voyaging, without food, hungrily, till they found (another) island, with a great cliff round it on every side, and therein was a long, narrow wood, and great was its length and its narrowness.

When Máel Dúin reached that wood he took (from it) a rod in his hand as he passed it. Three days and three nights the rod remained in his hand, while the boat was under sail, coasting the cliff, and on the third day he found a cluster, of three apples at the end of the rod. For forty nights each of these apples sufficed them.

VIII

Thereafter, then, they found another island, with a fence of stone around it. When they drew near it a huge beast sprang up in the island, and raced round about the island. To Máel Dúin it seemed swifter than the wind. And then it went to the height of the island and there it performed (the feat called) 'straightening of body', to wit, its head below and its feet above; and thus it used to be: it turned in its skin that is, the flesh and the bones revolved, but the skin outside was unmoved. Or at another time the skin outside turned like a mill, the bones and the flesh remaining still.

The Monster of the Feats.

When it had been for long in that wise, it sprang up again and raced round about the island as it had done at first. Then it returned to the same place; and this time the lower half of its skin was unmoved, and the other half above ran round and round like a millstone. That, then, was its practice when it was going round the island.

Máel Dúin and his people fled with all their might, and the beast perceived them fleeing and it went into the beach to seize them, and began to smite them, and it cast and lashed after them with stones of the harbour. Now one of these stones came into their boat, and pierced through Máel Dúin's shield, and lodged in the keel of the curragh.

IX

Now not long after that they found another lofty island, and it was delightful, and therein were many great animals like unto horses. Each of them would take a piece out of another's side, and carry it away with its skin and its flesh, so that out of their sides streams of crimson blood were breaking, and thereof the ground was full.

So they left that island swiftly, madly, hastily (and they were) sad, complaining, feeble; and they knew nothing whither in the world they were going and in what stead they should find aidance or land or ground.

X

Now they came to another great island, after great weariness of hunger and thirsting and they sad and sighing, having lost all hope of aidance. In that island were many trees: full-fruited were they, with great golden apples upon them. Red short animals like swine were under those trees. Now, they used to go to those trees and strike them with their hind-legs, so that the apples would fall from the trees, and then they would consume them. From dawn to sunset the animals did not appear at all, but they used to stay in the caverns of the ground. Round about that island many birds were swimming out on the waves. From Matins to None further and further they used to swim from the island. But from None to Vespers nearer and nearer they used to come to the island, and arrive therein after sunset.

Then they used to strip off the apples and eat them. 'Let us go', saith Máel Dúin, 'into the island wherein the birds are. Not harder for us (to do so) than for the birds'. *** One of the crew went to see the island, and he called his comrade to him on shore. Hot was the ground under their feet, and they could not dwell there for its warmth, because it was a fiery land, and the animals used to heat the ground above them.

The Red Hot Swine.

On the first day they brought with them a few of the apples which they were eating in their boat. When the morning was bright the birds went from the island swimming to sea. With that the fiery animals were up-raising their heads out of the, caves, and kept eating the apples till sundown. When they were put back into their caves the birds use to come in place of them, to eat the apples. Then Máel Dúin went with his people, and they collected all the apples that were there that night. Alike did the apples forbid hunger and thirst from them. So then they filled their boat with the apples as seemed good to them, and went again to sea.

XI

Now when those apples failed and their hunger and thirst were great and when their mouths and their noses were full of the stench of the sea, they sighted an island which was not large, and therein (stood) a fort surrounded by, a white, high rampart as if it were built of burnt lime, or as if it were all one rock of chalk. Great was its height from the sea: it all but reached the clouds. The fort was open wide. Round the rampart were great, snow-white houses. When they entered the largest of these they saw no one there, save a small cat which was in the midst of the house playing on the four stone pillars that were there. It was leaping, from each pillar to the other. It looked a little at the men, and did not stop itself from its play. After that, they saw three rows on the wall of the house round about, from one door post to the other. A row there, first, of brooches of gold and of silver, with their pins in the wall, and a row of neck-torques of gold and of silver: like hoops of a vat was each of them. The third row (was) of great swords, with hilts of gold and of silver, The rooms were full of white quilts and shining garments. A roasted ox moreover, and a flitch in the midst of the house, and great vessels with good intoxicating liquor. 'Hath this been left for us?' saith Máel Dúin to the cat. It looked at him suddenly and began to play again. Then Máel Dúin recognised that it was for them that the dinner had been left.

So they dined and drank and slept. They put the leavings(?) of the liquor into the pots and stored up the leavings(?) of the food. Now when they proposed to go, Máel Dúin's third foster-brother said: 'Shall I take with me a necklace of these necklaces?' 'Nay,' saith Máel Dúin, 'not without guard is the house'. Howbeith he took it as far as the middle of the enclosure. The cat followed them, and leapt through him (the foster-brother) like a fiery arrow, and burnt him so that he became ashes, and (then) went back till it was on its pillar. Then Máel Dúin soothed the cat with his words, and set the necklace in its place and cleansed the ashes from the floor of the enclosure, and cast them on the shore of the sea.

Then they went on board their boat, praising and, magnifying the Lord.

XII

Early on the morning of the third day after that they espy another island, with a brazen palisade over the midst of it which divided the island in two, and they espied great flocks of sheep therein, even a black flock on this side of the fence and a white flock on the far side. And they saw a big man separating the flocks. When he used to fling a white sheep over the fence from this side to the black sheep it became black at once. So, when he used to cast a black sheep over the fence to the far side, it became white at once. The men were adread at seeing that. 'This were well for us (to do)' saith Máel Dúin: 'let us cast two rods into the island. If they change colour we (also) shall change if we land on it'. So they flung a rod with black bark on the side wherein were the white sheep, and it became white at once. Then they flung a peeled white rod on the side wherein were the black sheep and it became black at once.

'Not fortunate(?) was that experiment,' saith Máel Dúin. 'Let us not land on the island. Doubtless ours colour would not have fared better than the rods'.

They went back from the island in terror. On the third day afterwards they perceived another island great and wide, with a herd of beautiful swine. therein. Of these they killed a small pig. Then they were unable to carry it to be roasted so they all came round, it. They cooked it and bore it into their boat.

Then they saw a great mountain in the island, and they proposed to go and view the island from it. Now when Diurán the Rhymer and Germán went to visit the mountain they found before them a broad river which was not deep. Into this river Germán dipped the handle of his spear and at once it was consumed as if fire had burnt it. And (so) they went no further. Then, too, they saw, on the other side of the river, great hornless oxen lying down, and a huge man sitting by them. Germán after this struck his spear-shaft against his shield. to frighten the oxen. 'Why dost thou frighten the silly calves?' saith that huge herdsman. 'Where are the dams of these calves' saith Germán. 'They are on the other side of yonder mountain,' saith he Diurán and Germán return to their comrades, and tell them the tidings.

So thence they (all) went.

XIV

Not long thereafter they found an island, with a great hideous mill, wherein was a miller huge *** hideous. They asked him 'what mill is this?'. 'Not *** indeed', saith he '*** asks what ye shall not know'. 'Nay' say they. 'Half the corn of your country,' saith he, 'is ground here. Every thing which is begrudged is ground in this mill saith he.

With that they see the heavy, countless loads on horses, and, human beings (going) to the mill and from it, again; only that what was brought from it was carried westward. Again they asked: 'What is the name of this mill? Inber Tre-cenand,' saith the miller. Then after this they signed themselves with the sign of Christ's cross. When they heard and saw all these things they went on their way, into their boat.

The Mill of Grudging.

XV

Now when they went from that island of the mill they found a large island, and a great multitude of human beings therein. Black were these, both in bodies and raiment. Fillets round their heads, and they rested not from wailing. An unlucky lot fell to one of Máel Dúin's two foster-brothers to land on the island. When he went to the people who were wailing he at once became a comrade of theirs and began to weep along with them. Two were sent to bring him thence, and they did not recognise him amongst the others (and) they themselves turned to lament. Then said Máel Dúin: 'Let four (of you)' saith he, 'go with your weapons, and bring ye the men perforce, and look not at the, land nor the air, and put your garments round your noses and round your mouths, and breathe not, the air of the land, and take not your eyes off your own men **** The four went, and brought back with them perforce the *** other two When they were asked what they had seen in the land, they would say: 'Verily, we know not, say they; 'but what we saw (others doing)' we did

Thereafter they came rapidly from the island.

XVI

Thereafter they come to another lofty island, wherein were four fences, which divided it into four parts. A fence of gold, first: another of silver: the third fence of brass: and the fourth of crystal. Kings in the fourth division, queens in a another, warriors in another, maidens in the other. A maiden went to meet them and brought them on land, and gave them food. They likened it to cheese; and whatever taster was pleasing to anyone he would find it therein. And she dealt (liquor) to them out of a little vessel, so that they, slept an intoxication of three days and three nights. All this time the maiden was tending them. When they awoke on the third day they were in their boat at sea. Nowhere did they see their island or their maiden.

Then they rowed away.

XVII

Thereafter they found another island which was not large. Therein was a fortress with a brazen door and brazen fastenings thereon. A bridge of glass (rose) by the portal. When they used to go up on the bridge they would fall down backwards. With that they espy a woman coming out from the fortress, with a pail in her hand. Out of the lower part of the bridge she lifts a slab of glass, and she filled the pail out of the fountain which flowed beneath the bridge, and went again into the fortress.

'A housekeeper comes for Máel Dúin!' saith Germán. 'Máel Dúin indeed', saith she, closing the door behind her.

After this they were striking the brazen fastenings and the brazen net that was before them, and then the sound which they made was a sweet and soothing music, which sent them to sleep till the morrow morning.

When they awoke they saw the same woman (coming) out of the fortress, with her pail in her hand and she fills (it) under the same slab.

'But a housekeeper comes to meet Máel Dúin! saith Germán.

'Marvellously valuable do I deem Máel Dúin!' saith she, shutting the enclosure after her.

The same melody lays them low then till the morrow. Three days and three nights were they in that wise. On the fourth day thereafter the woman went to them. Beautiful, verily, came she there. She wore a white mantle, with a circlet of gold round her hair. Golden hair she had. Two sandals of silver on her rosy feet. A brooch of silver with studs of gold in her mantle, and a filmy, silken smock next her white skin.

'My welcome to thee, O Máel Dúin!' saith she; and she named each man (of the crew) apart, by his own name. 'It is long since your coming here hath been known and understood.

Then she takes (them) with her into a great house that stood near the sea, and hauls up their boat on shore. Then they saw before them in the house a couch for Máel Dúin alone, and a couch for every three of his people. She brought them in one pannier food like unto cheese or táth. Sheer gave a share to every three. Every savour that each desired this he would find therein. There she tended Máel Dúin apart. And she filled her pail under the same slab, and dealt liquor to them. A turn for every three she had. Then she knew when they had enough. She rested from dealing to them.

'A fitting wife for Máel Dúin were this woman,' saith every man of his people.

Then she went away from them, with her one vessel and with her pail.

Said his people to Máel Dúin: 'Shall we say to her, would she, perchance, sleep with thee?'

How would it hurt you,' saith he, 'to speak to her? She comes on the morrow. They said to her: 'Wilt thou shew affection to Máel Dúin, and sleep with him? and why not stay here tonight?' She said she knew no sin, had never known, what sin was. Then she went from' them to her house; and on the morrow, at the same hour, comes with her tendance to them. And when they were drunken and sated, they say the same words to her.

'Tomorrow' saith she, an answer concerning that will be given to you. Then she went to her house, and they sleep on their couches. When they awoke they were in their boat on a crag and they saw not the island, nor the fortress, nor the lady, nor the place wherein they had been.

XVIII

As they went from that place they heard in the north-east a great cry and chant as it were a singing of psalms. That night and the next day till none they were rowing that they might know what cry or what chant they heard. They behold a high, mountainous island, full of birds, black and dun and speckled, shouting and speaking loudly.

They rowed a little from that island, and found an island which was not large. Therein were many trees and on them many birds. And after that they saw in the island a man whose clothing was his hair. So they asked him who he was, and whence his kindred. 'Of the men of Ireland am I', saith he. 'I went on my pilgrimage in a small: boat, and when I had gone a little from land my boat split under me'. I went again to land,' saith he, 'and I put under my feet sod from my country, and on it I gat me up to sea and the LORD stablished that sod for me in this place,' saith he, 'and God addeth a foot to its breadth every year from that to this, and a tree every year to grow therein. The birds which thou beholdest in the trees,' saith he, 'are the souls of my children and my kindred, both women and men, who are yonder awaiting Doomsday. Half a cake, and a slice of fish, and the liquor of the well God hath given me. That cometh to me daily,' saith he, 'by the ministry of angels At the hour of none, moreover, another half-cake and slice of fish come to every man yonder and to every woman, and liquor of the well, as is enough for everyone'.

When their three nights of guesting were complete; thy bade (the pilgrim) farewell, and he said to them: 'Ye shall all,' saith he, 'reach your country save one man'.

XX

On the third day after that they find another island, with a golden rampart around it and the midst of it white like down. They see therein a man, and this was his raiment the hair of his own body. Then they asked him what sustenance he used. Verily', saith he, 'there is here a fountain in this island. On Friday and on Wednesday whey or water is yielded by it. On Sundays, however, and on feasts of martyrs good milk is yielded by it. But on the feasts of apostles, and of Mary and of John Baptist and also on the hightides (of the year), it is ale and wine that are yielded by it'. At none, then, there came to every man of them half a cake and a piece of fish; and they drank their fill of the liquor which was yielded to them out of the fountain of the island. And it cast them into a heavy sleep, from that hour till the morrow. When they had passed three nights of guesting, the cleric ordered, them to go. So then they went forth on their way, and afterwards bade him farewell.

XXI

Now when they had, been long avoyaging on the waves they saw far from them an island, and as they approached it, they heard the noise of the smiths smiting a mass (of iron) on the anvil with sledges, like the smiting of three or; of four. Now when they had drawn near it they heard one man asking of another: 'Are they close at hand?' saith he. 'Yea saith the other. 'Who', saith another man, 'are these ye say are coining there?' 'Little boys they seem in a little trough yonder', saith he. When Máel Dúin heard what the smiths said, he saith: 'Let us retreat', saith he, 'and let us not turn the boat, but let her sterns be foremost, so that they may not perceive that we are fleeing

Then they rowed away, with the boat stern-foremost. Again the same man who was biding in the forge asked: 'Are they now near the harbour?' saith he. 'They are at rest', saith the watchman: 'they come not here and they go not there'.

Not long thereafter he asked again: 'what are they doing now?' saith he. 'I think', saith the look-out man, 'that they are running away; meseems they are further from the port now than they were some time ago', Then the smith came out of the forge, holding in the tongs a huge mass (of glowing iron), and he cast that mass after the boat into the sea; and all the sea boiled; but he did not; for they fled with all their warriors' might, swiftly hurried forth into the great ocean.

XXII

After that they voyaged till they entered a sea which resembled green glass. Such was its purity that the gravel and the sand of that sea were clearly visible through it; and they saw no monsters nor beasts therein among the crags, but only the _pure gravel and the green sand. For a long space of the day they were voyaging in that sea, and great was its splendour and its beauty.

They afterwards put forth into another sea like a cloud and it seemed to them that it would not support them or the boat. Then they beheld under the sea down below them roofed strongholds and a beautiful country. And they see a beast huge, awful, monstrous, in a tree there, and a drove of herds and the tree, and flocks round about the tree and beside the tree an armed man, with shield and spear and sword. When he beheld yon huge beast that abode in the tree he goeth thence in and flight. The beast stretched forth his neck out of the tree and sets his head into the back of the largest ox of the herd and dragged it into the tree, and anon devours it in the twinkling of an eye. The flocks and the herdsmen flee away, at once. and when

Máel Dúin and his people saw that greater terror and fear seize them, for they supposed that they would never cross that sea without falling down through it, by reason of its tenuity like mist.

So after much danger, they pass over it.

XXIV

Thereafter they found another island, and up around it rose the sea making vast cliffs (of water) all about it. As the people of that country perceived them, they set to screaming at them and saying: 'tis they! It is they!', till they were out of breath. Then Máel Dúin and his men beheld many human beings, and great herds of cattle, and troops of horses and many flocks of sheep. Then there was a woman from below with large nuts which remained floating on the sea, waves above by them, Much of those nuts they gathered and took with them. (Then) they went back from the island and thereat the screams ceased.

'Where are they now', saith the man who was after them at the scream. 'They have gone away' saith another 'band, of them'. 'They are not so,' saith another band.

Now it is likely that there was someone concerning whom they (the islanders) had a prophecy that he would ruin their country and expel them from their land.

XXV

They gat them to another island, wherein a strange thing was shewn to them, to wit, a great stream rose up out of the strand of the island and went, like a rainbow, over the whole island, and descended into the other strand of the island on the other side thereof. And they were lying, under it (the stream) below without being wet. And they were piercing (with their spears) the stream above; and (them) great, enormous salmon were tumbling from above out of the stream down upon the soil of the island. And all the island was full of the stench (of the fish), for there was no one who could finish gathering them because of their abundance.

From Sunday eventide to Monday forenoon that stream did not move, but remained at rest in its sea round about the island. Then they bring into one place the largest of the salmon, and they filled their boat with them, and went back from that island still on the ocean.

XXVI

Thereafter they voyaged till they found a great silvern column. It had four sides, and the width of each of these sides was two oar-strokes of a the boat, so that in its whole circumference there were eight oar-strokes of the boat. And not a single sod of earth was about it, but (only) the boundless ocean. And they saw not how its base was below, or because of its height how its summit was above. Out of its summit came a silvern net far away from it; and the boat went under sail through a mesh of that net. And Diurán gave a blow of the edge of his spear over the mesh. 'Destroy not the net', saith Máel Dúin, 'for what we see is the work of mighty men. For the praise of God's name', saith Diurán, 'I do this, so that my tidings may be the more believed; and provided I reach Ireland (this piece of the mesh) shall be offered by me on the altar of Armagh'. Two ounces and a half was its weight when measured (afterwards) in Armagh.

And then they heard a voice from the summit of yonder pillar, mighty, and clear, and distinct. But they knew not the tongue it spake, or the words it uttered.

XXVII

Then they see another island (standing) on a single pedestal, to wit, one foot supporting it. And they rowed round it to select way into it, and they found no way thereinto; but they saw down in the base of the pedestal, closed door under lock. They understood that that was the way by which the island was entered. And they saw a crowd on the top of the island; but they held speech with no one, and no one held speech with them. They (then) go away back (to sea).

XXVIII

After that they came to a island, and there was a great plain therein, and on this a great tableland heatherless, but grassy and smooth. They saw in that island near the sea, a fortress, large, high and strong and a great house therein adorned and with good couches. Seventeen grown-up girls were there preparing a bath. And they (Máel Dúin and his men) landed on that island and sat on a hillock before the fort. Máel Dúin said this: 'We are sure that yonder, bath is getting ready for us'. Now at the hour of none they beheld a rider on a race-horse (coming) to the fortress. A good, adorned horse-cloth under her seat: she wore a hood, blue and she wore a bordered purple mantle. Gloves with gold embroidery or, her hands; and on her feet, adorned sandals. As she alighted, a girl of the girls at once ok the horse. Then she entered the fortress and went into the bath. Then they saw that it was a woman that had alighted from' the horse, and not long afterwards came a, girl of the girls unto them. 'Welcome is your arrival!' saith she. 'Come into the fort: the queen invites you'. So they entered the fort and they all bathed. The queen sat on one side of the house, and her seventeen girls about her. Máel Dúin. sat on the other side, over against the queen, with his seventeen men around him. Then a platter with good food thereon was brought to Máel Dúin, and along with it a vessel of glass full of good liquor; and (there was) a platter for every three and a vessel for every three of his people. When they had eaten their dinner the queen said this How will the guests sleep? saith she. 'As thou shalt say', saith Máel Dúin. Your going from the island', saith she, 'Let each of you take his woman, even her who is over against him, and let him go into the chamber behind her'. For there were seventeen canopied chambers in the house with good beds set. So the seventeen men and the seventeen grown-up girls slept together, and Máel Dúin slept with the queen. After this they slumbered till the morrow morning. Then' after morning they arose (to depart). 'Stay here', saith the queen, and age will not fall on you, but the age that ye have attained. And lasting, life ye shall have always and what came to you last night shall come to you every night without any labour. And be no longer awandering from island to island on the ocean!

'Tell us', saith Máel Dúin, 'how thou art here'

'Not hard (to say), indeed', she saith. 'There dwelt a good man in this island, the king of the island. To him I bore yon seventeen girls, and I was their mother. Then their father died, and left no heir. So I took the kinship of. this island after him. Every day', she saith, 'I go into the great plain there is in the island, to judge the folk and to decide (their disputes)'.

'But why dost thou leave us today?' saith Máel Dúin.

'Unless I go', she saith, 'what happened to us last night will not come to. us (again). 'Only stay', she saith, 'in your house, and ye need not labour. I will go to judge the folk for sake of you'.

So they abode in that island for the three months of winter; and it seemed to them that (those months) were three years. 'It is long were here', saith one of his people to Máel Dúin. 'Why do we not fare to our country?' saith he.

'What you say is not good', saith Máel Dúin' for we shall not find in our own country aught better than that which we find here'.

(But) his people began to murmur greatly against Máel Dúin, and they said this great is the love which Máel Dúin hath for his woman. 'Let him, then, stay with her if he desires', saith the people. 'We will go to our country'.

'I will not stay after you', saith Máel Dúin.

One day, then, the queen went to the judging where into she used to go every day. When she had gone. they went on board their boat. Then she comes on her horse, and flings a clew after them, and Máel Dúin catches it, and it clung to his hand. A thread of the clew was in her hand, and she draws the boat unto her, by means of the thread, back to the harbour.

So then they stayed with her thrice three months. Then they came to (this) counsel. 'Of this we are sure, now,' saith his people, 'that great is Máel Dúin's love for his woman. Therefore he attends the clew, that it may cleave to his hand and that we may be brought back to the fortress'. 'Let some one else attend the clew', saith Máel Dúin, and, if it clings to his hand, let his hand be cut off'.

So they went on board their boat. (The queen came and) flung the clew after them. Another man in the boat catches it, and it clings to his hand. Diurán cuts off his hand, and it fell, with the clew, (into the sea). When she saw that, she at once began to wail and shriek, so that all the land was one cry, wail and shrieking.

So in that wise they escaped from her, out of the island.

XXIX

They were for a very long while afterwards driven about on the waves, till they found an island with trees upon it like willow or hazel. Thereon were marvellous fruits thereon, great berries. So of these then they stript a little tree, and then they cast lots to see who should prove the fruit that had been on the tree. (The lot) fell to Máel Dúin. He squeezed some of the berries into a vessel and drank (the juice), and it cast him into a deep sleep from that hour to the same hour on the morrow. And they knew not whether he was alive or dead, with the red foam round his lips, till on the morrow he awoke.

(Then) he said to them 'Gather ye this fruit, for great is its excellence'. So they gathered (it), and they mingled. water with it, to moderate its power to intoxicate and send asleep. Then they gathered all there was of it and were squeezing it and filling (with its juice) all the vessels they had; and (then) they rowed away from that island.

XXX

Thereafter they land on another large island. One of it two sides was a wood with yews and great oaks herein. The other side was a plain with a little lake in it. Great herds of sheep were therein. They beheld there a small church and a fortress. They went to the church. An ancient grey cleric was in the church, and his hair clothed him altogether. Máel Dúin asked him: 'Whence art thou?' saith he.

The Queen of the Magic Clew.

'I am the fifteenth man of the community of Brenainn of Birr. We went on our pilgrimage into the ocean and came into this island. They have all died save me alone'. And then he shewed them Brenainn's tablet, which they the monks had taken with them on their pilgrimage. The all prostrated themselves to the tablet, and Máel Dúin gave it a kiss.

'Now', saith the ancient man, 'eat your fill of the sheep, and do not consume more than sufficeth you'.

So for a season they are fed there on the flesh of the fat sheep.

One day, then, as they were looking out from the island they see (what they take to be) a cloud coming towards them from the south-west. After a while, as they were still looking, they perceived that it was a bird; for they saw the pinions waving. Then it came into the island and alighted on a hill near the lake. Then they supposed it would carry them in its talons out to sea. Now it brought with it a branch of a great tree. Bigger than one of the great oaks (was) the branch and large twigs grew out of it, and a dense top was on it (covered) with fresh leaves. Heavy, abundant fruit it bore red berries like unto grapes only they were bigger. So (the wanderers) were in hiding, awatching what the bird would. do. Because of its weariness, it remained for while at rest. (Then) it began to eat some of the fruit of the tree. So Máel Dúin went till he was at the edge of the hill on which the to see whether it would do him any evil, and it did bird was, ato that place gone. All his people then went after him.

'Let one of us go', saith Máel Dúin 'and gather some of the fruit of the branch which is before the bird'.

So one of them went and he gathers a portion of the berries and the bird blamed him not, and did not (even) look (at him) or make movement. They, the eighteen men, with their shields, went behind it, and it did no, evil to them.

Now at the hour of none of the day they beheld two great castles in the south-west, in the place whence the great bird had come, an d they, swooped down in front of the great bird. When they had been for a long while at rest, they began to pick and strip off the lice that infested the upper and, lower parts of the great bird's jaws, and its eyes and ears.

They (the two eagles) kept at this till vespers. Then the three of them began to eat the berries and the fruit of the branch. From the morrow morning till midday, they were picking the same vermin out of all its body and plucking the old feathers out. of it and picking, out completely the old scales of the mange. At midday, however they stripped the berries from the branch, and with their beaks they were breaking them against the stones and then casting 'them into the sea so that its foam upon it became red. After that the great bird went into the lake and remained washing himself therein nearly. till the close of the day. After that he went out of the lake and settled on another lace in the same hill, lest, the lice which had been taken out of him should come (again).

On the morrow morning the (two) birds with their bills still picked and sleeked the plumage (of the third), as if it were done with a comb. The kept at this till midday. Then they rested a little, and then they went away to the quarter whence they had come.

Howbeit the great bird remained behind them preening himself and shaking his pinions till the end of the third day. There at the hour of tierce on the third day he. soared and flew thrice round the island. and alighted for a little rest on the same hill. And afterwards he fared afar towards the quarter whence he had come. Swifter and stronger (was) his flight at that time than (it had been) before. Wherefore it was manifest to them all that this was his renewal from old age into youth, according to the word of the prophet, who saith 'Thy youth shall be renewed like the eagle's'.

Then Diurán, seeing, that great marvel, said: 'Let us go into the lake to renew ourselves where the bird has been renewed'.

'Nay', saith another, 'for the bird hath left his venom therein'.

'Thou sayest ill', saith Diurán, 'I the first will go into it'.

The Great Bird.

XXXII

Then he went in and bathes himself there and plunged the lips into (the) water, and drank sups thereof. Passing strong were his eyes thereafter so long as he remained alive; and not a tooth of him fell (from his jaw), nor a hair from his head; and he never suffered weakness or infirmity from that time forth.

Thereafter they bade farewell to their ancient man; and of the sheep they took with them provision. They set their boat on the sea, and then they seek the ocean.

XXXI

They find another large island, with a great level plain therein. A great multitude were on that plain, playing and laughing without any cessation. Lots are cast by Máel Dúin and his men to see unto whom it should fall to enter the island and explore it. The lot fell on the third of Máel Dúin's foster-brothers. When he went he at once began to play and to laugh continually along with the islanders as if he had been by them all his life. His comrades stayed for a long, long space expecting him, and he came not to them. So then they leave him.

After that the sight another island, which was not large; and a fiery rampart was round about it; and that rampart used to revolve round the island. There was an open doorway in the side of that rampart. Now, whenever the doorway would come (in its revolution) opposite to them, they used to see (through it) the whole island, and all, that was therein, and all its indwellers, even human beings beautiful, abundant, wearing adorned garments and feasting with golden vessels in their hands. And the wanderers heard. their ale-music. And for a long space were they seeing the marvel they beheld, and they deemed it delightful.

XXXIII

Not long after they had gone from that island they see far off among the waves a shape(?) like a white bird. They turned the prow of the boat unto it southward, to perceive what they beheld. So when they had drawn near it in rowing. they saw that it was a human being and that he was clothed only with the white hair of his body. He threw himself in prostrations on a broad rock.

When they had come to him, they entreat a blessing from him, and ask him whence he had gone to yonder rock.

'From Torach, verily', saith he, 'I have come here, and in Torach I was reared. Then it came to pass that I was cook therein; and I was an evil cook, for the food of the church wherein I was dwelling I used to sell for treasures and jewels for myself: so that my house became full of counterpanes and pillows and of raiment, both linen

and wool colour, and of brazen pails and of small brazen tellenna, and of brooches
of silver with pins of gold. Insomuch that unto my house there was nothing wanting
of all that is hoarded by man; both golden books and book-satchels adorned with
brass and gold. And I used to dig under the houses of the church and carry many
treasures out of them'.

'Great then was my pride and my haughtiness'.

'Now one day I was told to dig a grave for the corpse of a peasant, which had
been brought into the island. As I was (working) at that grave I heard. from below
me the voice out of the ground under my feet: 'But do not dig up that place!', saith
the voice. 'Do not put the corpse of the sinner on me a holy pious person!'.

'(Be it) between me and God, I will put (it)', say I, 'in my excessive haughtiness'.

'Even so', saith he. 'If you put it on me', saith the holy man, 'thou shalt perish on
the third day hence, and thou shalt be an inhabitant of hell and the corpse will not
remain here'.

Said I to the ancient man: 'What good wilt thou bestow me if I shall not bury the
man above you?'

'To abide in eternal life along with God', saith he.

'How', say I, 'shall I know that?'.

'That is neither hard nor for thee', saith he. 'The grave thou art digging will now
become full of sand'. Thence, wilt not be able to but will be manifest to thee that
thou art the man above me, (even) though thou buriest me'. That word was not
ended when. the grave became full of the sand. So thereafter I buried the corpse in
another. Now at a certain time set a new boat with tanned hide on the sea. I went on
board my boat, and I was glad. So I looked around me: and I left in my house
nothing from small to great, that was not brought by me, with my vats and wise lets
and with my dishes while I was in that looking. at the sea, and the sea was calm for
me great winds' come upon me, and draw me into the main, so that I saw neither
land nor soil. Here my boat became still, and thereafter it stirred not from one stead.
As I looked round me on every side, I beheld on my right hand the man sitting
upon. the wave. 'Then he said to me 'Whither goest thou' saith he. 'Pleasant to me
say, 'is the direction in which I am gazing over the sea now' It would not be
pleasant to thee, if thou keepest the band that surrounds thee. What may this band
be?' say I. Saith he to me: 'So far as thy sight. reaches over sea and up to the clouds
is one, crowd of demons all around thee, because of thy covetousness and thy pride
and haughtiness, and because of thy theft and thin other evil deeds. Knowest thou',
saith he, 'why thy boat stops?' 'Verily, I know not'. 'Thy boat shall not go out of
the place wherein it stand until thou do my will. 'Mayhap I shall not endure it', say
I. 'Then thou wilt endure the pains of helplessness til you endure my will'. He came

me towards me then, and lays his hand on me; and duly promised to do his will.
'Fling' said he, 'into the sea all the wealth that thou hast in the boat'. 'It is a pity',
say I, 'that it should go to loss'. It shall in no wise go to loss. There will be one
whom thou wilt profit. (Then) I fling every thing into the sea, save a little cup. Go
now saith he to me, and forth the, stead in which thy boat will pause stay therein
And then he gave. me for. provision a cup of whey-water and seven cakes. So I
went', saith the ancient man, 'in the directions that my boat and the wind carried
me: for I had platform oars and my rudder. As I was there then, a tossing among, the
waves, I am cast upon this rock, and then I doubted whether the boat had stopt, for I
saw neither land nor soil here. And I remembered what had been said, namely, to sit
in the' sea where my boat should stop. So I stood up and saw a little crag, against
which the wave beat. Then I set my foot, on that little crag, and my boat escapes
from me and the crag I lifted me up, and the waves withdrew. Seven years am I
here', saith he '(living) on the seven cakes and on the cup of whey-water which was
given me by the man who sent me from him. And I had no (provision) save only
my, cup of whey-water. This still remained there. After that I was in a three days
fast', saith he. 'Now after my three days, at the hour of none, an otter brought me a
salmon out of the sea. I pondered in my mind that it was not possible for me to eat a
raw salmon. I threw it again into the sea', saith he, 'and I was fasting for another
space of three days. At the third none, then, I saw an otter bring the salmon to me
again out of the sea, and another otter brought flaming firewood, and set it down,
and blew with his breath, so that the fire blazed thereout. So I cooked the salmon,
and for seven other years I lived in that wise. And every day', saith he, 'a salmon
used to come to me, with its fire, and the crag increaseth so that (now) it is large.
And on that day seven years my salmon is not given me: (so) I remained I am
(fasting) for another space of three days. At the third none of the three days there
half a cake of wheat, and a piece of fish were cast up. Then my cup of whey-water
escapes from. me and came to me a cup of the same size filled with good liquor
which is on the crag here and it is full every day. And neither wind, nor wet, nor
heat, nor cold affects me this place. Those are my narratives saith the ancient man..
Now when the. hour of none arrived, half a cake and a piece of fish come to each of
them all, and in the cup which stood before the cleric on the rock was, found their
fill of good liquor. Thereafter said the ancient man to them Ye will all reach your
country, and the man a that slew thy father, O Máel Dúin, you will find him in a
fortress before you. And slay him not, but forgive him because God hath saved you
from manifold great perils, and ye too are men deserving of death Then they bade
farewell to the ancient man and went on their accustomed way

XXXIV

Now after they had gone thence they come to an island with abundant cattle, and
with oxen and kine and sheep. 'There were no houses nor forts therein, and so they
eat the flesh of the sheep. Then said some of them seeing a large falcon there: 'The
falcon is like the falcons of Ireland!' That is true indeed', say some of the others.
'Watch it' saith Máel Dúin, and see how the bird will go from us. They saw that it

flew from them to the southeast. So they rowed after the bird, in the direction in which it had gone from them. They rowed that day till vespers. At nightfall they sight land like the land of Ireland. They row towards it. They find a small island and it was from this very island that the wind had borne them into the ocean when the first went to sea.

Then they put their prow on shore, and they went toward the fortress that was in the island, and they were listening, and the inhabitants of the fortress were then dining.

They heard some of them saying: 'It is well for us if we should not see Máel Dúin

'That Máel Dúin has been drowned', saith another man of them.

'Mayhap it is he who will wake you out of your sleep', saith another man.

'If he should come now', saith another, 'what should we do?'

That were not hard (to say) saith the chief of the house: 'great welcome to him if he should come, for he hath been for a long space in much tribulation'.

Thereat Máel Dúin strikes the clapper against the door valve. 'Who is there?', saith the doorkeeper.

'Máel Dúin is here', saith he himself. 'Then open!' saith the chief, 'welcome is thy coming'.

So they entered the house, and great welcome is made to them, and new garments are given them. Then they, declare all the marvels which God had revealed to them according to the word of the sacred poet who saith Haec olim meminisse iuuabit. Máel Dúin (then) went to his own district, and Diurán the Rhymer took, the five half-ounces (of silver) which brought from the net, and laid them on the altar of Armagh in triumph and in exultation at the miracles and great marvel which God had wrought for them. And they declared their adventures from beginning to end, and all the dangers and perils they had found on sea and land.. Now Aed the Fair, chief sage of Ireland, arranged this story as it standeth here; and he did (so), for delighting the mind and for the folks of Ireland after him.

Made in the USA
Middletown, DE
12 November 2022

14792334R00076